D1621932

Humble and Strong

HUMBLE
AND STRONG

MUTUALLY ACCOUNTABLE LEADERSHIP
IN THE CHURCH

Gerald W. Keucher

Morehouse Publishing
NEW YORK · HARRISBURG · DENVER

Copyright © 2010 by Gerald W. Keucher

All rights reserved.

Unless otherwise noted, the Scripture quotations contained herein are from the New Revised Standard Version Bible, copyright © 1989 by the Division of Christian Education of the National Council of Churches of Christ in the U.S.A. Used by permission. All rights reserved.

Morehouse Publishing, 4775 Linglestown Road, Harrisburg, PA 17112
Morehouse Publishing, 445 Fifth Avenue, New York, NY 10016
Morehouse Publishing is an imprint of Church Publishing Incorporated.
www.churchpublishing.org

Cover design by Laurie Klein Westhafer

Library of Congress Cataloging-in-Publication Data
Keucher, Gerald W.
Humble and strong: mutually accountable leadership in the church / Gerald W. Keucher
    p.   cm.
ISBN 978-0-8192-2408-8 (pbk.)
ISBN 978-0-8192-2436-1 (e-book)
1. Christian leadership. 2. Leadership—Religious aspects—Christianity.
I. Title.
BV652.1.K48 2010
248.8'92—dc22

                                                    2010017966

Printed in the United States of America

10 11 12 13 14 15   10 9 8 7 6 5 4 3 2 1

*With love and gratitude to
the people and staff of the Church of the Intercession
New York City*

What is impossible for mortals is possible for God.

(LUKE 18:27)

CONTENTS

ACKNOWLEDGMENTS

FOR SEVERAL YEARS I have led a session for Episcopal seminarians on the church's disciplinary canons, which are the procedures outlined in church law that must be followed in cases of alleged misconduct against clergy. In addition to explaining the relevant parts of the canons, I have also presented handouts that contain a rudimentary version of both the pitfalls discussed in Chapter 3 and the preventive measures outlined in Chapter 4. The response of the students to the material I have been presenting gave me the idea that a book like this might be useful. I am grateful to them for their interest and feedback.

I came at this book from another direction as well. Over the years I have met with hundreds of vestries and groups of lay and clergy leaders to talk about financial leadership and strategic management of assets by churches and not-for-profits. I began to see that giving people the tools to do a reasonable analysis of their situation was not sufficient. If the leaders, lay or ordained, were not good at being leaders, nothing of value would happen. Only good leaders could look at the institution's condition and make appropriate, dispassionate, long-range decisions about how to improve it. I thank all those people who were part of all those meetings. I learned something from each and every one.

I'm grateful to the Rev. Canon William F. Geisler, CPA, Controller Emeritus of the Diocese of California and a consultant with the Church Pension Group. His tax and financial planning seminars for clergy have taught me much, and his friendship has meant a great deal.

I would like to thank Frank Tedeschi and Cynthia Shattuck of Church Publishing, Inc. for their faith in this book and for their patience in helping me get it to this state. I eagerly acknowledge the assistance of the friends with whom I have discussed the ideas here and who read versions of the manuscript and made valuable suggestions: Patrick Williams, Michael Rebic, and the Reverends Nora Smith, Bob Shearer, John Merz, Lucia Lloyd, Chuck Howell, and Fred Johnson.

Families come in different varieties, and I am grateful for mine—for John, my partner of thirty-three years, for my mother who has made her home with us in her retirement, for Marsha and Marcel, and now little Natalie and Mia. Becoming Grandpa Jerry has been a life-changing experience I never expected to have.

And I am profoundly grateful to the clergy and laypeople with whom I have been privileged to work. This book references situations when leadership hasn't gone so well, but there are lots of humble and strong leaders out there whose examples have taught me what to avoid.

I hope what follows is of use to the leaders of the church I love.

Staten Island, New York
Feast of Saint Barnabas the Apostle
June 11, 2010

INTRODUCTION: LEADERSHIP AS CRAFT

WHAT MAKES A good leader? In talking about good leadership we need to begin with a prior and more basic question: what kind of person do you need to be in order to become a good leader? How can you become that kind of person so you can become that kind of leader?

I want to suggest that effective leadership is not a skill set that can be taught to anyone, as one can be taught how to make a hardboiled egg without cracking the shell or how to swing a thurible. You don't become an effective leader by memorizing a list of do's and don'ts, or by simply resolving to handle your time or your staff differently. Least of all do you become an effective leader simply because you have attained a position of leadership.

I'd like to suggest that coming to be an effective leader is more like becoming proficient in a foreign language or mastering a musical instrument. In our junior year a high school classmate asked me if I would teach her how to play "Rhapsody in Blue." I asked her if she could play the piano. She said she couldn't, but that it wasn't important because she didn't want to learn; she just wanted to play "Rhapsody in Blue." I was unable to persuade her that she couldn't play George Gershwin's masterpiece without first learning to play the piano. One might as well desire to reproduce the Mona Lisa without learning how to draw or paint.

I think the analogy is apt because becoming a good leader, like becoming a good violinist or linguist, involves practicing lots of little things that may not seem directly connected to the final goal. We may never find ourselves needing to say, "Where is the pen of my aunt?" but we will need to ask the way to the ATM or the subway; we will need to be able to call up the right forms of the verb "to be"; and we will no doubt speak of writing and family relationships, though perhaps not together. If we don't have the component parts of vocabulary and syntax in our heads and on our tongues, we won't be able to put the sentence together that fits the occasion. Like taking part in a conversation, leadership is intensely relational, and good leadership speaks to a specific situation like an apposite remark.

I think being a good leader means having practiced the vocabulary and syntax of the craft so we can put together the expression of leadership needed at a particular moment in a particular relationship. It is no more helpful to say, "In a situation like this, I always do that" than it is to say, "When someone asks me where the bathroom is, I always say, 'to the left.'" A good leader's response to a situation will be appropriate for that situation and maybe it won't be the same as in other situations that are somewhat similar to it. My rule of thumb is that rules of thumb must not be followed slavishly.

Now let me press the analogy a bit further. The question is this: what kind of person do we need to be to be a good leader? It might be useful to think about what kind of person we need to be to play the violin, speak Italian, or practice cabinetry. I think at the most basic level there must be a willingness to respect the otherness of what you're learning. You can't translate English idioms into Spanish; you have to learn the Spanish ones. You can't ask why Italian is not like English or try to make it work like English; you have to start thinking like an Italian. In other words learning any craft requires a certain abnegation of self. It's not about you; it's about submitting yourself to a complex body of pre-existing material, discovering connections, and finding delight in the material itself. Mastery was perhaps our goal at the outset, but we soon discover that mastery is a byproduct of the work we have done for the love of the craft.

This is an especially important point for leaders. As I have said, we don't become good leaders just because we have been appointed or elected to a leadership position. However, the lack of structural and personal accountability in the church's systems means that many who achieve leadership roles never learn how to be effective leaders. No one is in a position to tell them their deficiencies, and should someone try, it's easy not to pay attention but rather to accuse the truth-teller of inappropriate conduct. So in many religious and secular organizations there are in tenured or contracted leadership positions the equivalent of a violinist who is unable to bow or finger, or a linguist who cannot conjugate verbs. The lack of leadership competence has negative effects on the health of the institution, of course, but lack of self-awareness, and the defensiveness that results from a glimmer of unwanted self-awareness, do the real damage.

Cabinetmakers produce furniture, musicians produce performances and recordings, and the legacy of good leaders is a future for the institution they lead. The most important job you have as a leader is to prepare for your successor, as a former bishop of mine always said. Another friend recently put it this way, "You are responsible for the success of your successor." If it all falls apart when you leave, it sounds like you didn't prepare for your successor that well. Maybe you were doing it all yourself, so there was no one ready to step up. Maybe the institution was really in a seriously weakened state, but you had been successfully maintaining the outward impression that everything was fine.

We are responsible both to those who bequeathed us the institutions we lead, and to those who will inherit them from us. The decisions we make don't have to do only with present circumstances; we always need to ask whether it is respectful of our history and if it prepares us for a stronger future. Abnegation of self is really called for here. It truly is not about us—and the more we think it is, the poorer the job we'll do of preparing for our successors.

THE NEED FOR MUTUAL ACCOUNTABILITY

Some years ago I was having a tense conversation with a higher-up who at one point exclaimed to me, "I'm not accountable to you!" Difficult as that conversation and that relationship were, I am grateful for them because that statement prompted me to articulate for the first time what has become the guiding idea in this book. I said, "Relationships that are not mutually accountable are abusive."

We will have occasion to explore this fully. We learn much by watching others, but leadership is best learned by leading. If we are in a leadership position before we have mastered the craft, we have much to learn, but we cannot learn it if we do not hold ourselves accountable to those we lead. Books, workshops, and seminars are all useful in the way learning a language in school is useful, but we will need some big adjustments when we take our classroom knowledge into the streets. We will need to learn much from those with whom we speak. If we're not eager to have native speakers give us feedback, we will never improve our accent or speak idiomatically. This was brought home to me when, during his summer internship in this country, a Hungarian intern with good classroom English skills asked me, "What does 'Hah-doon?' mean?" I finally had to ask *when* people said it to her. Of course it was how her co-workers greeted her each day, but in class she had not learned that the five syllables of "How are you doing?" get elided into two in colloquial speech.

In a church or organization, the feedback we need is from those we are leading—the staff, the board, the volunteers, and the members. Some of the feedback may not be helpful, but most of it can be. We will not benefit from it unless we cultivate an atmosphere of trust that allows those who work for and with us to speak their minds. We have many ways of deceiving ourselves into thinking that we are doing fine when all we've really done is to figure out ways of not letting people tell us the things we really need to hear. We will examine many of these methods of self-deception along the way.

Both before and after ordination, in government and not-for-profit organizations as well as the church, I have had the opportunity to observe and experience a variety of leadership styles. Even the ones that could not be characterized as effective were useful in the sense that what doesn't kill us makes us stronger. Some of the stories I've seen and heard will be, I hope, illustrative of the points I intend to make.

How We Will Proceed

The questions with which this book deals are these: What kind of person do we need to be to be an effective leader, and how do we become that kind of person? The thesis of this book is in two parts. First, to be effective, leadership must be humble and strong. Second, the key to effective leadership is two-way relationships, that is, relationships of true mutual accountability between leaders and those they lead. The purpose of this book is to analyze these claims and then to discuss how those who are preparing to be leaders, as well as those who wish to be more effective leaders, can develop habits and patterns of life that will help humility and strength to become second nature.

Chapter 1 will examine the context in which leadership is exercised today, a context that is undergoing change. For example, churchgoers will easily cross denominational lines to find a community with which they feel an authentic connection. This makes good leadership even more important because bad leadership will impede the formation of that connection at a time when weakened institutional loyalties create an "authority problem." Authenticity and authority are now very closely related. I will also point out the differences between effective leadership, which is always selfless, and charismatic leadership, which is always self-centered.

Chapter 2 will make the case, first of all, that effective leadership is humble and strong, and second, that such leadership is always characterized by mutual accountability. One-way relationships are abusive, a strong but not always self-evident claim. Chapter 3 goes on to outline some of the pitfalls we can encounter and the ways they can distort our leadership into something arrogant, weak, and unaccountable. Some of these pitfalls are problems we create for ourselves by making inappropriate adaptations to the circumstances of ministry. For example, some clergy develop dangerous practices around handling money because the vestry has refused to reimburse necessary business travel. Bad things happen when simple, basic fairness is lacking. Our vocation also suffers because of the baggage we brought with us to ministry, such as a tendency to rely too much on charm and to bring too little substance to our work.

Chapter 4 lists some practices that I believe will help us become the kind of people who can exercise humble and strong leadership. Some are measurable suggestions like reading the daily office; others might be called habitual *intentions* we can develop, like apologizing frequently. It is my belief that all these suggestions will have an effect in making you the kind of person who can be a good leader.

Finally I will offer some very practical advice on the role of the vestry and the role of the rector. I think most leadership imbroglios come about because people are either not fulfilling the duties or overstepping the boundaries of their role. The short form of the advice is that vestries do governance and the rector and staff do management. There can be only bad outcomes when vestries cede their governance function to an overbearing rector, or when a vestry tries to do management.

Speaking of management, I will also offer what I hope are helpful guidelines on how to supervise staff. There is a difference between supervision and friendship, just as there is a big difference between supervision and pastoral care. As long as professional boundaries are maintained at work, it's fine to be friends with co-workers and subordinates, and there will almost certainly be times when you will need to minister to your staff as you minister to parishioners. However, neither friendship nor pastoral care can substitute for good supervision. There are ways of demonstrating to staff that you trust them and that you value their contributions, and this almost always inspires people to give their very best to the service of the institution.

A bishop once startled a diocesan convention by remarking that we do not learn from experience. After a pause, he continued, "We learn from *reflection* on experience." My hope is that the reflections recorded here will assist in your own reflections on what you have seen and done, and so help inform your thoughts about what you'd like to do and how you'd like to go about it.

CHAPTER ONE

THE CONTEXT
OF LEADERSHIP

*Only that which does not teach, which does not cry out,
which does not persuade, which does not condescend, which
does not explain, is irresistible.* —William Butler Yeats

WHEN A CONGREGATION stumbles, there may be various
external reasons that include changing demographics, financial
setbacks or large-scale recession, and shifts in private and public
funding for programs. Congregations generally stumble, however,
because of internal factors such as conflict, depleted endowments,
or serious deferred maintenance. Leadership, however, is always
critical. A congregation can fail to thrive even with good leadership
if the members are in constant conflict, the building problems are
overwhelming, or if there are insurmountable external factors. No
matter how favorably a congregation is situated, however, I have
never seen one thrive without leadership that is humble and strong.

Yet does humble and strong leadership really matter that
much? Despite Jesus' example, throughout history there have
certainly been Christian leaders who were arrogant, ambitious,
narcissistic, and careless. Individuals may not have liked them
personally, but the institution of the church continued to do
well. I think that humble and strong leadership especially matters
today, however, because of two related factors.

First, belonging to a church is now truly voluntary. For the first time people are in church only because they want to be. Christendom, a society in which Christianity is favored by social and legal pressures, is no more. Long gone are any norms or social expectations encouraging church attendance in most parts of this country; if anything, social pressure now goes the other way and it is not unusual for churchgoers to feel a bit apologetic about being observant when they are with their non-churchgoing friends.

Since people now go to church only because they are searching for something, some religious leaders complain about a consumer mentality that has taken over. The church must now offer the "product" the consumer wants, so the grumbling goes. I think this charge is largely unfair: people come to church because they are looking for things like meaning, connection, community, an authentic experience of God, opportunities to serve others and to confront injustice, the healing of past hurts, and the beauty of holiness. They do not come to see and be seen or to satisfy superficial lifestyle choices. This means that when they come, they need to find signs that the life-transforming experiences we advertise are authentically on offer.

If this is a bad thing, we really have only ourselves to blame. We relied so much and for so long on the threat of hell that it lost its force. We tried to control people's actions and to limit the scope of their inquiry, but the fear of punishment and the threat of social ostracism no longer works except in highly controlled and sectarian communities. Personally I think it is appropriate to rejoice that we are done with the distractions and distortions that come with conformity to social and cultural orthodoxy. To be sure, our current position requires some significant adjustments. If we were living in a church-going culture, we wouldn't have to spend time talking about why people do, or might want to, go to church; it would be one of the givens of the culture. In that situation we can rely on cultural norms and social pressure to get the people inside the door.

In a post-Christian and secular culture, however, we can assume nothing. There will be no familiarity with bible stories or church ways. A young woman told me once that she had been "raised lapsed Catholic," meaning that she had been baptized but had never been to church. Her children may well not be baptized. If this woman and her children are going to be evangelized, it won't be on the basis of threats of punishments or promises of rewards, both of which create the same unhelpful psychological dynamic. Hectoring, didactic, doctrinaire approaches are not going to work.

Instead, such people will seek out the church either because they have perceived some kind of longing or desire, or they have felt something is missing. A colleague who has taught comparative religion in private schools observes that when someone wants to be a Buddhist, she learns spiritual disciplines and practices. In Christian inquirers' classes, however, the emphasis is mostly on history, doctrine, and what makes our particular tradition superior. I think that those who come to us are looking for connection rather than correctness. The idea that in each of us there is a "God-shaped hole" is a useful way of describing how many experience their spiritual seeking. The church's history and creeds are important, but they are secondary. First comes some kind of sense that here you can find what your soul longs for—seekers need to apprehend that God can be met and experienced here. Good leadership is vital in making the community open enough and patient enough to let seekers move at their own speed.

Another way of describing this search is to say that people are responding to the pull of what Yeats calls "the irresistible," something that does not teach, cry out, persuade, condescend or explain. What would a presentation of the gospel look like that did not depend first on catechesis, oratory, systematic argument, authoritative teaching, or explanation? There will be plenty of time for all these necessary activities once someone has responded to the pull of the irresistible. Our normal ways of trying to teach, persuade, or threaten seekers into relationship with God have proved quite easy to resist.

In the Acts of the Apostles, it is Christians' lives that are the irresistible attraction. When the jailer in Philippi sees that Paul and Silas have not escaped from prison despite being freed by the earthquake, he asks, "What must I do to be saved?" (Acts 16:30), which I think can be interpreted as, "How can I become like you?" Those who have found the God-shaped hole in themselves and those who are responding to the gentle tug of the irresistible need to apprehend somehow that the connection they seek can be found in our communities.

This may be a way of bridging the gap that has developed in recent years between "spirituality" and "religion," whereby people increasingly define themselves as "spiritual but not religious." The definitions of spirituality vary, but it seems fair to say that people use "spirituality" to speak of what feels like an authentic interior experience, while "religion" is taken to mean the organized beliefs and ritualized observances of a group of people. A common perception on the part of those who don't attend church seems to be that "religion" is all rules and outward practices that tend toward the exclusion of other paths to God. This perception is often warranted because churches frequently present the beliefs and the rules first, and are not shy about making exclusivist claims.

It might be that if, in our dealings with seekers, we pastors were attentive to the inner experience that has brought the person to us, we might not have to persuade and convince. We don't have to waterboard people with doctrine. When people can speak of their longing and their experience, catechetical formation won't need to be imposed; they will ask for it because they'll want to satisfy their thirst for the living water.

THE PROBLEM OF AUTHORITY

The fact that the church is now truly a voluntary association where seekers expect to find authentic Christianity means there also has to be a change in how the church is led. The kind of top-down leadership no longer works that worked when the church was assumed to be part of the general culture and institutional affiliation was much more important than it is now. People are suspicious of traditional authorities, so to speak about how leadership in the church has to change we need to look briefly at changing concepts of power and authority.

Power is the ability to do something, including making someone else do something. Power at its most basic resides in the brute strength necessary to accomplish certain outcomes; a mob has the power to kill a perceived criminal, for example. Authority is different. It is power that is *conferred* within a community of people in a way the community views as legitimate. In our community courts, not mobs, have the legitimate power to punish wrongdoers. If people are in any kind of community, they must share to some extent a common source of authority; if people look to the same source of authority, they are by definition part of a community.

The conferral of authority in a community may be informal, so that the group recognizes someone as wise or experienced enough to be tacitly given certain powers. Extended families and groups of friends often confer authority in this way. Informal authority can be found in the workplace alongside of, or even in opposition to, the organizational chart. Parishes, especially family-sized ones, frequently operate through informal authority: no matter who's on the vestry, Betty still calls the shots. Many contemporary megachurches in effect confer authority informally by recognizing the founding pastor who originally gathered the congregation as the legitimate leader.

Some informal conferral of authority is almost universal in human groups. In a group of three or four friends, one will likely be acknowledged informally as the sparkplug that gets things going, the one whose opinion the others seek out. Because these situations are unstructured, there can be trouble if the group grows beyond a certain size. Then people begin to question how eligibility for leadership is determined, how leaders are selected, how long they serve, and what happens when the leader needs to be replaced. There can be, and frequently are, troubles when the informal ascription of authority proves inadequate to the size or complexity of the organization, or when it is necessary to provide for a successor to the leader. When those founding pastors try to make their position hereditary, rough sailing is often the result.

Communities usually have a formal structure that confers certain powers on a person by virtue of the position she holds in the community. For example, the powers of the presidency are conferred by the constitution and by statute on the president. On taking office the president is authorized to exercise those powers. The larger the community and the longer it has existed, the more likely it is to have a formal structure of authority with rules that provide who can choose the leaders and what powers they are authorized to exercise and for how long. As the community becomes an institution, the more likely it is that its members will come to believe that simply by achieving a certain position one can exercise effectively the powers that come with the office.

It was probably never really sufficient for a leader to say, "Because I'm in charge and I said so," and certainly not today. Authority, remember, is a combination of power and legitimacy. When institutional loyalties are weaker, you don't get the legitimacy you need just from being chosen in accordance with the rules. The ability to exercise effectively, the power of an office, no longer comes automatically with the office; it must be earned. Certainly a new rector or a new bishop will begin with a reservoir of goodwill and will usually be cut some slack as he or she settles in. However, that reservoir will be quickly drained by a few high-handed or careless actions. If those continue, the leader will find herself still able to exercise the powers of her office, but she will not have the kind of *influence* that inspires and moves hearts. She will not get the cooperation necessary to move the organization forward because her leadership lacks the kind of legitimacy necessary to elicit it.

Most church leaders, like the leaders of many membership organizations, do not have a lot of executive authority. They can't move the organization they lead through their efforts alone. The members are volunteers, not staff that can be fired. Leaders must work with semi-autonomous auxiliaries, committees, boards, and related agencies, all of which have their own constituencies and interests. Leaders must inspire and gain the trust of these bodies in order to accomplish anything. That is what I mean by saying that influential authority is now absolutely necessary to effective leadership. The former National Executive Director of the Girl Scouts, Frances Hesselbein, when asked in an interview how she accomplished so much without concentrated executive power, replied, "Oh, you always have power, if you just know where to find it. There is the power of inclusion, and the power of language, and the power of shared interests, and the power of coalition. Power is all around you to draw upon, but it is rarely raw, rarely visible."[1]

What Hesselbein is saying is that for leadership to be effective, the authority that comes with the office must be accompanied by the informal recognition among the people that this person authentically embodies the community's values and aspirations. In other words institutional legitimacy is not enough for effective leadership; the leader must also be regarded as a worthy occupant of the office.

WHEN LEADERSHIP FAILS

In fiercely contested presidential campaigns people sometimes say, "If X is elected, I'm moving to Canada!" The moves rarely take place, however, for two reasons. In general we trust our constitutional structures sufficiently that we will put up with an administration we can't abide, both because we'll get another chance in four years and because we have term limits. Besides, although the president is an important figure, our everyday lives take up more mental space than our preoccupation with the national government.

In many churches, however, there are no terms limits for the ordained leadership; rectors can stay indefinitely, and bishops have life tenure. We have no built-in safety valve. People don't know when the leader will leave, and it's usually pretty messy to try to get rid of a settled minister. Churches are different in another way as well—few organizations hold a membership meeting every week. Inadequate leadership can't be ignored when it's in front of you every Sunday. I imagine we have all had the experience of attending services led by someone whose leadership we simply cannot respect. It is not pleasant, and we will generally try not to undergo the experience very often. We may not move to Canada because X is elected president, but we are likely to vote with our feet and leave when church leadership disappoints or disillusions us.

This sense of disillusionment is not wholly new. Christians have always struggled with the discrepancy between our talk and our actions. They aspire to show forth in their lives what they profess by their faith, and want no less from their leaders. At certain points in their history Christians' dissatisfaction with poor leadership has threatened schism, as when the Donatists of the fourth century decided that the ministries of bishops and priests who had renounced their faith under persecution were invalid, and barred them from repenting and returning to their leadership positions. The anti-clerical Lollard movement of fourteenth-century England focused on the corruption of the Roman Catholic Church, its leaders and its ties to government. Both these movements were related to the perceived "unworthiness" of the ministers and the church of their day.

The church's response to complaints about the unworthiness of the minister is both theologically correct—that the validity of the sacraments does not depend on the worthiness of the minister—and exactly what one would expect an institution to say. A priest in a state of mortal sin can still administer a valid baptism or eucharist because the sacraments depend on God's action, not on individual merit. Indeed, who is worthy to lead the Lord's people? Yet the institutional convenience of the position is also obvious.

Most people, I think, could be brought to understand and agree conceptually with this position. It would be an administrative nightmare, and impossibly subjective, to try to monitor the "worthiness" of all the clergy. Nevertheless, on the ground such monitoring occurs regularly among the faithful, while people seem less and less willing to accept the ministry of one who comes across as inauthentic, high-handed, or hypocritical. They'll go to another parish or simply stop attending church. If they stay because of their love for the parish, they may reduce their giving or attend less frequently, and certainly won't respond with enthusiasm to anything the leader proposes.

Thus some members of the church seem to agree with the church's position in the abstract, but in real life act like the Donatists and refuse the ministrations of those they deem unworthy. I do not say this as a criticism. Some parishioners, of course, do become disaffected for superficial or self-serving reasons, but a priest who preaches, say, on the joys of marriage while going through a messy public separation from his wife can cause real offense. This is a scandal in the original sense of the word—behavior that is a stumbling block in the path of the congregation's journey of faith. They cannot hear whatever merit there might have been in the sermon because the preacher's words are so much at odds with the his life. In such a situation faithful people are right to be scandalized.

If Christians have never liked unworthy ministers, why is it more urgent than ever that leaders not be unworthy? Here are some factors that appear to me to be different. The large mainline denominations are those that benefited most from Christendom, the social arrangement that rewards church participation. The Episcopal, Presbyterian, Lutheran, Congregationalist, and Reformed churches are the descendents of various forms of the established church in Europe and in colonial America. These denominations have been slow to adjust to a situation in which church participation is truly voluntary. Other denominations, like the Methodists and Baptists, are also affected by the disappearance of a churchgoing culture. At the same time, many of the churches mainline congregations worship in are older buildings of architectural distinction; for example, half of the fifty Episcopal churches in Manhattan are either individually designated New York City landmarks or are located within historic districts. The church has, in effect, undertaken an open-ended commitment to maintaining a particular set of structures whose builders did not design them to last centuries. In addition such plants depend on endowments for their maintenance, and endowments have not always been handled well.

I can tick off a list of parishes in this area of the country—some of national renown—that have recently been in such weakened condition that if the vestry had called one more mediocre or incompetent leader, they would have closed. This prospect focused the minds of the vestries, and in each case they called a rector who is now working doggedly to turn the place around. This would be hard enough if all they had to contend with were social trends and aging buildings, but when you add the past mismanagement that depleted the endowments, deferred the maintenance of the buildings, and left a lasting rancor in parish dynamics, such work is challenging indeed. Nor are small, rural churches exempt. Parish leaders of all kinds have to work to undo past mistakes, inspire a hope in a new future, and be able to offer seekers the possibility of finding the connection they long for.

The damage done by bad leaders is harder and harder to repair. A bad leader can easily weaken a parish, but can almost never kill one outright through his or her efforts alone. However, absent external pressures that keep pews filled, parishes are less resilient than they used to be and can exist in something close to a persistent vegetative state.

Charisma is not the Point

By now you might be thinking that far too much emphasis is being placed on the character or personality of the leader, but that is not the same thing as "charismatic leadership." In his book on leadership entitled *Good to Great*, Jim Collins makes the point that charisma is not only dangerous in a leader, but also a liability, and he defines the highest form of leadership as *humility* plus *will*. The charismatic leader's strength of personality, he writes, "can sow the seeds of problems, when people filter the brutal facts from you." Such a leader can become the reality driving the company, and "the moment a leader allows himself to become the primary reality people worry about . . . you have a recipe for mediocrity, or worse."[2] In the church disaster, not mediocrity, is often the result of charismatic leadership.

People with charisma become used to bending others to their will with little trouble, and so they come to feel that they are entitled to have their way. Believing all the adulatory comments their admirers make, they feel that they deserve to be surrounded only by people who are impressed by their magnetic personalities. Such leaders are usually bad for the future of an organization; they tend to think only of what they want, rather than of what is in the best long-term interests of the institution they lead. Thus they will frequently urge that endowments be spent on projects they want, alienate or drive away those who don't respond to their personalities, and view others as competitors for the limelight rather than as colleagues in service to the mission of the organization. In one instance an outstanding and remarkably collegial organist was dismissed by the new priest, who said to her, "I hear you're a 'star' and I don't want 'stars' in my administration." I think the priest actually meant that there could be only one star.

Getting to the Starting Line

As we have already seen, leaders cannot rely on their position in the organization to give them the authority they need to be effective, nor should they rely on the force of their personalities to give them that authority. Leaders must find ways of always being approachable so that those they lead can tell them the truth. I know for a fact that this kind of accessibility inspires people to give the very best of which they are capable. People will happily go far beyond their job descriptions if they feel those they work for are really listening and care what they think; then they know they are a valued member of a team that is doing worthwhile work.

Barriers to good leadership include our need for ego gratification, our tendency to personalize disagreement and fix blame, and our attachment to one-way relationships that can easily become abusive. Unless we overcome these tendencies, we become someone our co-workers, subordinates, and members have to manage around. In such situations the people you lead cannot focus on the most effective way to do the job; they must think first about how to get your attention, how to make their case to you without you getting defensive, and how to work around you while watching their backs. This dynamic drains a good bit of energy from the organization; people will not give their best and morale will be extremely low. No matter how often you tell your staff that you're all part of a team, everybody knows that the dynamics are those of a dictatorship. You'll end up like the priest who, after a lengthy sermon on servant leadership was preached at his institution, said to the senior warden at the reception, "Now I'm the rector, and you have to do what I say!"

My purpose here is to help us do the soil preparation necessary to make it possible for the suggestions, approaches, and recommendations in this and other books on leadership to take root and grow. This book does not outline a theory or philosophy of leadership, but it does have one main underlying principle: the less a relationship is characterized by mutual accountability, the more it tends to become abusive. One-way relationships are dangerous for both parties, whether we're talking about spouses, parents and children, supervisors and subordinates, or priests and parishes. For me this principle is integral to any discussion of humility and strength. Leaders who do not conscientiously maintain two-way relationships with those they lead will simply not be effective. My intent is to remain as close as possible to the motivations, relationships, and dynamics I think most of us have experienced or seen. The goal here is to help us recognize the warning signs more quickly and take remedial action while there is still time.

A Small Study

Perhaps you are thinking that I'm overstating the situation and perhaps the problem of good leadership is not all that great. To attempt an answer I looked at the history of leadership since 1977 in the ten congregations of a county I know well. In that time there have been thirty-four "settled ministers"—that is, rectors or vicars/priests-in-charge with renewable contracts. I did not include interims or supply clergy. In 1977 all ten parishes had settled clergy; at present three are in interim situations, so of the thirty-four, seven are incumbents while twenty-seven left their positions between 1977 and 2009. One of those twenty-seven died in active service, and here is what happened to the remainder:

- Four suffered breakdowns of different types and had to be removed. These were uniformly messy situations that did great damage to the congregations before and after the removal.
- Five resigned or retired under pressure from the vestry or the diocesan office. The vestry of one congregation gave the rector a substantial financial incentive to go.
- Six more left in circumstances where there was significant disappointment or discontent on one or both sides.

In other words, nine, or more than one-third, of the clergy were essentially forced out, while another six of the departures were less than happy. Thus the tenure of fifteen of those twenty-six priests ended unhappily, and five of those fifteen had gotten stuck—they had stayed far beyond the point where their ministries were no longer effective. All were unable for various reasons to find another cure, although at different points in their tenure they had tried to do so. Obviously none of the fifteen priests who departed in unhappy circumstances left their parishes stronger than they were when they arrived.

Of the remaining eleven, eight did very good jobs, as did the priest who died, leaving their congregations in markedly better shape than at their arrival. Membership, attendance, and annual giving were up. There was a vital program life, and the buildings were being taken care of.

It isn't possible to say that the strong cultural and social headwinds of a secular society are to blame for such a record, because throughout the entire period, the congregations of the priests who provided good leadership did well. Nor did some of the parishes always do well while others steadily declined. Each of the ten congregations had or has at least one good leader, and every time the congregation had a good leader it revived. Each also had at least one period during which a weak leader caused the congregation to stumble.

The seven current incumbents, most of whom are fairly new in their positions, are all good and effective priests, working hard and doing well. However, it is also true that at least six of the nine clergy whose tenure ended very badly did a good job in the first years of their ministries. Things changed as they got stuck or developed other problems that led to the unhappy ends.

It is not possible to extrapolate percentages from this small sample to all of the mainline denominations or even to the Episcopal Church. Nevertheless, I think the following points are important and do apply more broadly:

- All of these parishes grew and thrived when they had good leadership.
- None of them did well when good leadership was lacking.
- Fewer than one-third of the past leaders provided that good leadership throughout their tenure.

Such a record also raises questions about the adequacy of oversight. I'm not talking about "lowering the boom"; the bishop's office removed people when things had deteriorated completely. But is that "sink or swim" approach the right one? Does it make sense to let such situations get to that point, or to keep doing the same things while expecting different results? Such a small case study doesn't prove anything, but it might indicate that more of the decline of the mainline churches is due to internal failures of leadership and oversight at both the parish and the diocesan level than it might be comfortable for us to acknowledge.

In the next chapter I will examine what I mean by these key words, humility and strength. Nowadays "humility" has come to mean either low self-esteem or a form of hypocrisy that pretends to think you are less than you are. I would like to set forth what I think is a biblical and traditional understanding of humility, to recover a Christian virtue I think we need more of. Similarly, what often seems like "strength" to a leader is experienced by others as overbearing rigidity, unwillingness to listen, or a stubborn refusal to admit mistakes. So our understanding of strength also needs some work. Finally, we will examine some of the common barriers we erect to keep ourselves from practicing strong humility, and come to find that humility and strength, as I understand them, are two sides of the same coin.

End Notes:

1. Jim Collins, Good to Great (New York: HarperCollins, 2001), 10.
2. Ibid, 72–73.

CHAPTER TWO

HUMILITY AND STRENGTH

For by the grace given to me I say to everyone among you not to think of yourself more highly than you ought to think, but to think with sober judgment. (Rom. 12:3)

Only the gentle are ever really strong. —James Dean

IN ONE OF the first confirmation classes I taught, I discovered that for all the young people in the class, "humility" meant either believing that you are worse than you are or pretending to believe that you're worse than you are. "Pride" meant feeling good about yourself. My students had no equivalent for "a proper estimation of one's talents and abilities" and they used other expressions such as "full of herself," or "stuck on himself" for "an excessively high opinion of oneself; excessive self-involvement."

Humility, as I understand it, is neither genuine nor feigned self-abasement, but an appropriate, accurate estimation of one's abilities and accomplishments. This kind of self-knowledge can often look like self-abasement, however, because our innate tendency is to think more highly of ourselves than we should or to overestimate our abilities. For example, three-quarters of drivers think they are safer than the average, and two-thirds believe they are more skillful than the driver of average skill. But if we truly saw ourselves as we are, using St. Paul's "sober judgment," or as others see us, our humility might look like abasement to many.

15

Humility does not mean a lack of self-confidence, however. For who is as confident as one who truly knows what her capacities and limitations are? Humility does not mean making yourself a doormat, but the confidently humble will be likely to respond differently from the arrogant and the unsure. Going the second mile, offering the other cheek, heaping coals of fire on the heads of one's enemies by doing them good, overcoming evil with good—these are neither platitudes nor the ways of weakness or arrogance. These are responses to difficulties that only the humble can make, embodying the weakness of God that is stronger than human strength.

How do we acquire an appropriate gauge of our gifts? How do we know the opinion of our abilities we've come to is accurate? What are the things we do that keep us from getting that knowledge? Why isn't it easier for us to see ourselves as others see us?

HUMILITY IS ACCURATE SELF-KNOWLEDGE

Most of us don't do a very good job of seeing ourselves as others see us. How could we? We see ourselves as *we* do, and deceive ourselves so easily that we can't rely on our own self-examination. Besides, since we are social creatures seeking to lead an organization or a community, it is necessary that our estimation of our gifts and our behavior be informed by how they appear to others. Florence Foster Jenkins, a New York socialite who gave recitals for over thirty years despite her notable inability to sing, seems truly to have believed that she was among the great sopranos and that those who laughed at her performances were motivated solely by jealousy. Generations after her death, the discrepancy between her own opinion of herself and the perceptions of others still provides amusement, even on YouTube. This is an extreme example, but if our own estimation of ourselves is not informed by how others experience us, the results can be just as off-key. Worse still, we can do real damage to real people, and weaken the institutions we have been called to lead. So we need to find ways to hear from others that what we might consider in ourselves tact and diplomacy is seen by others as passive aggressiveness, for example, or that our commitment to the right way of doing things is experienced by those around us as a fierce need to control.

We will not find out what others think unless we cultivate relationships with friends, peers, and subordinates that allow us to hear the truth of their experience of us. Many people in charge do not welcome such relationships, but unless we make the effort to cultivate them, the higher we go in an organization, the less likely we will be to hear the truth. The less uncomfortable truth we hear, the more our ears are filled with the echoes of our own self-satisfaction and the compliments of self-seekers who hope to get something from us.

I do not mean that we simply accept the positive or negative opinions of others without further examination. If people express themselves freely, they will have wildly contradictory opinions of our qualities of leadership, some fair and some unfair. It is always easier to listen to those whose opinion agrees with our own self-evaluation. If we want to be effective leaders, however, we will want to listen to different voices and to take them into account.

I've heard clergy say, "Well, 95 percent of my people are great; there are just a few that don't like me." I've thought that myself, but the best leaders realize that it is a dangerous simplification. People can be abrupt, angry, and hurtful as they tell us their truth about us, which leads us to feel defensive and angry, but a humble leader does not act from spite or anger. A leader who is humble and strong—that is, a leader who has already received enough honest feedback to have gained a fairly accurate picture of herself—has enough self-confidence to consider, after the emotions die down a bit, whether there was anything in what was said that she particularly needs to hear. And if we give people appropriate, ordinary, everyday opportunities to tell us their truth about us, explosions of pent-up frustration become less likely.

STRUCTURES OF ACCOUNTABILITY

If any community is to last for very long, it requires a structure. Truly communal arrangements have always been small and have not survived for any period of time, much less over generations.

St. Francis of Assisi was dismayed by what happened to his order of friars as it grew, but if an institutional structure had not been created, his vision could not have spread and endured, despite the later failings of the institution his followers created. It seems that the treasure of which St. Paul speaks (2 Cor. 4:7) needs to be held in earthen vessels, the way angel food cake batter needs the right pan. It is also possible to set up structures of institutional accountability, like the checks and balances among the branches of the federal government, or regular elections and term limits. We can guarantee that someone is fairly selected for a position, that there are procedures for removal in cases of egregious wrongdoing, and no matter how good a job the leader has done, that the time will come, because of term limits or retirement, when the office will be vacated.

However, it is impossible to structure an organization to ensure that the leaders are personally accountable to those they serve. The only way a leader can understand how he is truly experienced by others is by voluntarily and deliberately setting up ways of ensuring that he will hear the truth. An insecure or arrogant person in any position will find ways to circumvent such safeguards, and being insecure or arrogant is of itself not sufficient cause for removal. However, the damage such leaders do is difficult to repair when they are gone. It is therefore desirable for leaders to create structures or avenues of communication so that colleagues, subordinates, and parishioners feel confident that they can tell us things we may not wish to hear without fear of reprisal. This is not limited to large organizations; in very small parishes people can feel that it would not be safe for them to say anything to the cleric or to a lay leader, even if his behavior is having a negative effect on the health of the congregation.

Many denominational structures do not have much in the way of institutional accountability. In most hierarchical or connectional denominations, the pastoral relationship of minister to congregation involves the judicatory, and the relationship can't be ended simply by a vote of the parish board. Even congregational churches usually require a vote of the membership to terminate the relationship, and that's more difficult than a vote by the board. In the Episcopal Church rectors and bishops have tenure, though it has become easier in recent years for a vestry to dissolve the pastoral relationship with the rector. In many ways this system is preferable to one in which deployment is handled solely by the bishop's office, because not all bishops are good leaders. Performance evaluations of parish clergy are a very touchy subject, and with good reason—lay leaders or diocesan officials may have their own agendas. But the price we pay for our system, which to some degree protects many clergy from arbitrary and capricious dismissal, is that some leaders stay in place long after they have become ineffective or, worse, destructive, because they are accountable to no one. In situations like this, endowments are depleted, building problems are ignored or repaired improperly, and the congregation dwindles as person after person becomes disaffected. Thus it is all the more necessary for clergy with tenure to make sure they develop mutually accountable, two-way relationships; otherwise they can become quite unapproachable and fail to create a climate where the truth can be heard. If you are already the kind of person who wants to be in relationships of true mutual accountability, you are probably already practicing similar techniques. The goal of this book is to foster the self-examination and possibly the conversion necessary to make us into people who want to hear the truth and confront the brutal facts.

POWER CORRUPTS

When Lord Acton, British historian and devout Roman Catholic, formulated his famous dictum about power in 1887, he was writing of the church, in particular his inability to accept the dogma of papal infallibility:

> I cannot accept your canon that we are to judge Pope and King unlike other men with a favourable presumption that they did no wrong. If there is any presumption, it is the other way, against the holders of power, increasing as the power increases. Historic responsibility has to make up for the want of legal responsibility. Power tends to corrupt, and

absolute power corrupts absolutely. Great men are almost always bad men, even when they exercise influence and not authority: still more when you superadd the tendency or certainty of corruption by authority. There is no worse heresy than that the office sanctifies the holder of it.

It is important for all leaders to order the organizations they lead so that they remain personally accountable to their employees, volunteers, and institutional structures.

Part of the challenge is that our good intentions and performance in other roles are not necessarily good indicators of what kind of leaders we will be. When a friend of mine who was renting an apartment bought a two-family house, he discovered that a complete shift from a tenant's to a landlord's mentality happened immediately upon signing the closing documents. Our perspective changes with our situation in ways that we are not entirely in control of. Over time, my tenant-turned-landlord friend took on some of the characteristics of his former landlords that he had always complained about. Yet he was unaware of it, so when it was pointed out to him, he thought the criticism was unfair. His former perspective had simply vanished, and he had no idea that his perspective had ever been different. I have heard priests complain about how they had been treated as curates while treating their own assistants just as badly.

When they do not feel accountable to those they serve, it is not unusual for parish clergy to exert such bullying control that they prevent the lay people who have fiduciary responsibility from exercising it. In one parish, the rector over the years spent the endowment down from several millions to less than $100,000—and then retired. He had not stolen money; he had simply done what he wanted with it, using it to complete unneeded capital projects and to plug increasing budget deficits instead of doing the hard work of stewardship formation and good institutional fundraising. When meeting with the vestry after his departure to start to help them get back on their feet, I asked a question about the management of their finances. Sitting next to me was an elderly woman whose family had attended the church for several generations, who whispered, "We weren't allowed to talk about these things." Imagine the dynamics that had to have existed for well-meaning, mature, successful adults to feel that they weren't allowed to ask the questions necessary to exercise the responsibilities given them by law and canon. Perhaps you don't have to imagine it; perhaps you've experienced it.

This is a good example of the dangers of one-way relationships and how they become abusive. First, they distort the vocation and even the personality of the leader to the point where there is no opening for truth to enter. Second, they damage the people who were the recipients of the abuse, who have to choose between leaving a congregation they love or staying and tacitly agreeing not to fulfill their fiduciary responsibilities. The spiritual and institutional recovery necessary in the aftermath of such a leader is complicated by the fact that the people who stayed were in effect forced to collude with a bad situation. The anger they feel toward the leader is mixed with a kind of shame and guilt at their own participation. Such relationships damage and can even destroy the institution the leader was charged with serving.

Finally, there is a further complicating factor. Usually it is people from the office of the judiciary, whether bishops, district superintendents, or other staff, who need to work with the congregation on its recovery. In most such situations the congregation feels that the judiciary let them down by allowing the situation to continue for so long. Since frequently those in authority could have at least brought some kind of leverage to bear, the congregation is more right than wrong, and the episode becomes one more example of why the congregation feels justified in continuing to distrust the judiciary.

SERVANT LEADERSHIP

Servant leadership is a phrase that has been around the church since the publication in 1977 of Robert K. Greenleaf's acclaimed book *Servant Leadership: A Journey into the Nature of Legitimate Power and Greatness*. I referred above to the long sermon on servant leadership that preceded the new rector saying to the wardens, "Now I'm the rector, and you have to do what I say."

It was sort of a joke, but it sort of wasn't. The damage done during his relatively brief, unhappy tenure and his tumultuous departure was certainly not funny at all. The important thing to remember about servants is that, of all people, they are always completely accountable to those they serve. Servants are told what to do, so if no one can tell you what to do, you are not a servant but a master. So if you want to think of yourself as a servant leader, it is all the more important that you find ways to hold yourself accountable to those you lead—and not just to those who admire you and whom you like. And please do not talk about yourself as a servant leader in a meeting or from the pulpit. Let others attribute that quality to you if you evince it; it isn't necessary to claim it for yourself. The phrase may be close to running its course in any case because of the skepticism many feel when the wrong people use it. It almost begins to seem as though those who hold themselves the least accountable are the ones who congratulate themselves the most about their servant leadership.

One of Greenleaf's main theses is that the organizational model that calls for a "single chief" is unsustainable:

> To be a lone chief atop a pyramid is *abnormal and corrupting*. None of us is perfect by ourselves, and all of us need the help and correcting influence of close colleagues. When someone is moved atop a pyramid, that person no longer has colleagues, only subordinates. Even the frankest and bravest of subordinates do not talk with their boss in the same way that they talk with colleagues who are equals, and normal communication patterns become warped. Even though a man or woman may have had a long record as an acceptable colleague with equals, on assuming the top spot that person will often become "difficult" (to put it mildly) to subordinates. The pyramidal structure weakens informal links, dries up channels of honest reaction and feedback, and creates limiting chief-subordinate relationships that, at the top, can seriously penalize the whole organization.[1]

Greenleaf nails the problem just as Lord Acton did ninety years earlier. One-way relationships are the norm when there is one person in charge. Leaders who would like to portray themselves as servant leaders have generally not grappled adequately with Greenleaf's critique of the "single chief" system. Quite often, therefore, the subordinates of those leaders have to deal with both the normal warped communication patterns of this system as well as the leaders' self-satisfied illusion that they are acting as servants.

However, Greenleaf's solution to the problem he analyzes so clearly is in my view vague and unworkable. Instead of a chief, he envisions a *primus inter pares*, a "first among equals" at the head of the operation of the organization. In addition, he envisions a board of trustees to oversee the management or governance of the institution. The board would be headed by another "first among equals" and it would have its own staff to provide adequate oversight of the operational side. Perhaps there are human cultures in which people are formed to be able to work within such structure. In a culture like ours, however, in which so many people are competitive, territorial, and insecure, I think Greenleaf's structure would simply not survive the continual battles it would engender. It is certainly not the model that prevails, certainly in the church. Tying your organization up in knots until what you consider the perfect organizational model is in place might actually be a mechanism to avoid confronting some of the "brutal facts" that may be threatening your organization. And paying too much attention to restructuring might really be an attempt to extend your control. Difficult as it is, maybe it is best to figure out how to operate as effectively as we can, with humility and strength, in the organizational model we already have.

When our organizational model is working in a healthy way, there is no single chief. Most churches are set up with some kind of board (vestry, session, council) and executive director (rector, pastor, senior minister). As in all not-for-profit corporations, the board is supposed to carry out governance while the executive director is accountable to the board and responsible for the management of the organization. That is to say, the board members are fiduciaries responsible for the real estate, buildings, and financial assets of the organization. They are responsible for setting policy and for hiring or calling the executive director, while management is to see to the program and the rest of the staff.

But this model often does not function in a healthy way. Boards frequently feel incompetent to deal with their fiduciary responsibilities and would rather criticize the cleanliness of the Sunday school room. The rector or minister frequently arrogates to herself the functions of governance and wants the board to act as a rubber stamp. The key point is that no one person or one group is supposed to run everything. It is not so much that there is supposed to be a balance of power between the board and the minister; rather, there are different roles each is to fulfill. The two need to be able to work together in mutually accountable ways, but their primary responsibilities are different. This is important enough that we will devote a chapter of this book to an in-depth examination of the responsibilities of each and how to develop and maintain a good working relationship.

"JERRY? THIS IS FATHER JONES."

English, unlike many of other languages, has lost the use of the familiar second-person pronoun "thou" and has only one form of the word "you." Other languages like German and Spanish have two forms for "you," one used with friends and intimates, the other in more formal settings. Each language has its own rules for when to use which form: in general, the informal address corresponds to situations when we would use someone's first name (intimates and peers), while the formal is used when we would (or should) use a title and surname—in cases where there is a difference of status or position. In those languages it is unheard of to use the informal form with a subordinate while requiring the subordinate to use the formal form with you, except when an adult is addressing a child or, in the old days, servants or peasants. So in Italian, for example, you use formal address with those whose position is either below or above yours, and you give a title both ways. It is a way of showing respect to those with both more and less power than you.

Yet even today many clergy want others to address them with a title like Father Bob, Mother White, Bishop Jones, or Pastor Mary while calling parishioners and staff by their first names. By doing this, you are not just putting yourself on a different level in the power structure, but setting yourself up as a different order of human being, one so far superior to those around you that you can give yourself permission to be informal with them but require formality *from* them. For example, when I worked at a diocesan office, occasionally another priest would call and say, "Jerry? This is Father Jones." The first time I was truly nonplussed. The second time it happened, I said in (I hope) a friendly, conversational tone, "If I'm Jerry, you're Bill. If you're Father Jones, I'm Father Keucher."

I can think of several ways to respond to the situation I'm describing. First, you might think this is not a problem. Your view may be that others should give you a title and that you should be able to use their first names. Or perhaps you justify it by thinking that you're not doing it for your own sake, but so that people will show proper respect for your office. Perhaps that is true, even though Jesus clearly had a different conception of the office of spiritual leader when he washed his disciples' feet.

By definition there cannot be a two-way relationship when one party in the relationship requires that the signs of respect flow in only one direction. It creates a constraint that becomes increasingly difficult to get past, because in every exchange the inequality of the relationship is reinforced no matter how friendly the conversation. Those in the subordinate position will think more than once about how honest they can be with someone who insists on setting up a relationship of inequality on this very basic level. If you as rector ask others to use your title without being formal in return, it is, I think, at the very least, a red flag warning that your effectiveness as a leader is at risk. You must work doubly hard to make sure you hear the truth from others.

When I recently tried these thoughts out on a group of divinity students, one told me that his bishop introduces himself, apparently modestly, by his first name, as in, "Hi, Bill. I'm Mark." He then expects others to respond, "Pleased to meet you, Bishop Jones." No doubt the bishop thinks he's being very approachable, but his seminarian experienced the move as a way of keeping him off balance and of making sure he was aware of the power dynamics. So if you want others to give you a title, you should use a title in return. Although it is difficult to sound old-fashioned

in today's society without seeming arch or ironic, irony is preferable to making others treat you like a feudal lord while you
presume to be informal in return.

Given the informality of our culture, I think it's best to go
with first names all around. Now, the situation may be out of
your hands, as many churchgoers have deep respect for the clerical
office and want to give a title to the priest while being called by
their first names. If the parishioner wants to give you a title yet be
called by his first name, do it, but please don't get too comfortable
with it. It really isn't good for anyone to get used to a relationship
of unequal respect with another adult.

ABUSIVE? REALLY?

I said before that the more a relationship lacks mutual accountability the more it tends to become abusive. Perhaps you thought
this was an overstatement. Perhaps you were put in mind of Mike
Godwin's 1990 law on inappropriate rhetoric: "As [an internet]
discussion grows longer, the probability of a comparison involving Nazis or Hitler approaches one." I've seen people hurl the
Nazi analogy during the second volley of an internet conversation, on a church listserv of course, and people do seem more
likely to use the language of violence, particularly sexual violence,
to describe dynamics unrelated to sex or violence. The head of
ministry development in one diocese said that people who reap-
ply for ordination after being turned down should be treated like
stalkers, the analogy being that the Commission on Ministry
is like a woman who has said no. Therefore to ask repeatedly is
seen as not just inappropriate, but threatening. To me this is an
example of rhetorical overkill, though perhaps I think that mostly
because it took me several applications to get ordained!

I think we do need to be careful of the language we use so
we do not demonize others just because we disagree with their
opinions. For example, I will not characterize it as hate speech if
you express your conviction that same-sex marriages should not
be blessed by the church, no matter how much I might disagree
with you. We should also be careful of our analogies. Seeking

ordination from the church is not like trying to get a date with someone who doesn't want to go out with you. It just isn't.

Can the one-way relationships that are so common in our workplaces and in churches be accurately described as abusive? One-way relationships are not all the same, and some are certainly more extreme than others. Most people who like to be called Father Bill and call others by their first names will not be like the rector that bullied his congregation into silence while he depleted the endowment. Let's examine this further.

As a part of the baptismal liturgy in the Episcopal Church, we affirm that with God's help we will respect the dignity of every human being. No doubt we have wondered how it is possible for us to repeat those words half a dozen or more times a year and still flatter some people and put down others—or at least we've wondered how other people can. I don't think this is due to sheer hypocrisy or utter obliviousness. Whatever we might think, what we are actually doing is ascribing a different level of dignity to different human beings depending on their status. After all, that is a possible interpretation of the words themselves. One of the meanings of the word "dignity" is "relative standing" or "rank," as in "moving tables and chairs is beneath my dignity." So we can think that we are respecting the dignity of every human being by treating them according to the level of dignity we think they are due, so administrative assistants deserve one level of respect and executives another. I don't think this is deliberate; it seems to happen on some instinctual level—as in communities of animals that have, literally, a pecking order. So it is natural for us to treat our superiors with a higher level of respect than we do our subordinates.

Thus the tradition of the Bible introduces something unnatural into the way we conduct interpersonal relationships. Surely the meaning of the words of the baptismal covenant is that every human being has exactly the same level of dignity. To respect the dignity of every human being cannot mean to accord each person the level of respect we think they deserve; rather it is to treat every person with the same measure of respect, and the level of respect we would wish to receive. This is difficult, and it is not in accord with the way we are formed and socialized.

Throughout the entire Bible, concepts of partiality, favoritism, and the perversion of justice that comes from taking status into account when rendering judgment appear scores of times in Exodus, Leviticus, Deuteronomy, 1 Samuel, 2 Chronicles, Job, Psalms, Proverbs, Ecclesiastes, Isaiah, Amos, Malachi, Sirach, 1 Esdras, Matthew, Mark, Acts, Romans, Galatians, Ephesians, Colossians, 1 Timothy and James. The most common biblical Greek and Hebrew expressions for showing partiality (*prosōpon lambano* and *nś' pnym*) mean literally "to receive face," that is, "to take appearances into account."

Almost every part of the Hebrew and Christian scriptures express a similar idea: God "shows no partiality," nor should we. In scripture "showing partiality" means to accord different levels of respect and different kinds of treatment to different people.

In the book of Acts and in the epistles, Jews and Gentiles, slaves and free persons, rich and poor, and male and female are on an exactly equal footing in the eyes of God. When the author of Acts has Peter proclaim, "I truly understand that God shows no partiality, but in every nation anyone who fears him and does what is right is acceptable to him. You know the message he sent to the people of Israel, preaching peace by Jesus Christ—he is Lord of all" (Acts 10:34–37), the early Christian communities are trying to take in the astonishing realization that all the former ways of classifying people are null and void. Gentiles can no longer be shunned, for, as Peter says later in Acts, "If then God gave them the same gift that he gave us when we believed in the Lord Jesus Christ, who was I that I could hinder God?" (Acts 11:17) Masters and slaves must relate to each other with the awareness that whatever either does, they will receive the same from the Lord, because both "have the same Master in heaven, and with him there is no partiality" (Eph, 6:9). Nor can the rich be shown deference while the poor are treated with disdain (James 2:1–4).

When the New Testament speaks against favoritism or partiality, it exults in God's revelation in the person of Jesus of the fundamental equality of each human person. Showing partiality, therefore, is a rejection, a denial of what God has done. Of course, the early church did not completely embody this equality any more than later generations of Christians, but that in no way negates the revelation. It simply means that the church must over and over repeat the pattern of slowly realizing that whatever groups we are excluding now must also be included.

In the Old Testament the emphasis is on justice, as we can see in the laws covering the treatment of widows, children, and resident aliens. God does not want the poor to be judged any differently from the rich. In the Hebrew scriptures, the evil of making distinctions between one person and another is usually grouped with bribes or flattery (Deut. 16:19; Job 32:21; Prov. 28:21). Taking bribes, currying favor, and making distinctions between people of different economic or social status are viewed by Scripture as a perversion of justice and corruption of character.

What happens to us when we abuse the trust of our office? Perhaps the first few times we might feel self-conscious or guilty, but with practice the conscience is hardened, and we may come to feel, through that strange perversion of the mind that corruption facilitates, that we are actually entitled. In the same way, we may at first feel a little self-conscious about requiring others to address us as "Bishop" or "Father" while presuming to use first names in return, but with practice we come to feel, through that same strange perversion of the mind, that we are entitled to treat those below us as lesser beings while we curry favor with those above us. In a very real sense, every person, and especially every leader, is like an elected official. God has entrusted us all with the care of our fellow creatures, and we abuse God's trust when we show partiality, use flattery, and demand signs of respect and deference that we feel we don't have to give in return. Having abused God's trust, it is really a very small step to abusing those to whom we think we are not accountable. The question is not whether we have ever treated someone we have some power over in a way that we would not wish to be treated—of course we have. The question is whether we have come to feel comfortable doing that.

If we have, we don't always end up with the reign of terror of that rector to whom I have referred. However, even mild-mannered leaders who practice one-way relationships can end up taking actions of breathtaking brutality and stunning stupidity against those they think are less important than they. From the point of view of those over whom we have power, it is always a kind of reign of terror to be under someone to whom they know they cannot speak the truth. If someone wants to keep her job, or stay a member of the parish she loves, then she must learn to let the truth go unspoken, to practice servile flattery, to swallow heedless, or even intentional, insults, and constantly to apologize for oversights and mistakes for which her leader was responsible. She may not be physically or sexually abused in such a situation, but the psychological dimensions of this kind of treatment are quite similar. Indeed, in my experience those who have experienced physical or sexual abuse will be especially wary of finding themselves in any one-way relationship because the psychological dynamics are just too similar.

THE NEED FOR CERTAINTY

All leadership positions are full of choices and therefore full of opportunities to get it wrong. Parishes perhaps have more opportunities for leaders to get it wrong than many other places, because you can make mistakes on so many fronts, from building maintenance and capital campaigns to sermons, liturgical style, and your relationships with lots of people. Most of us begin by sincerely wanting to do a good job. As it becomes apparent how many different enterprises there are that require our resources, however, and how many things the people expect us to be experts on, we can be intimidated. Moreover, the criticism we receive from vestry members and parishioners can get under our skin. We want to do the right thing, and when there are so many things we can get wrong and get criticized for, it's only human to try to find a way we can feel certain that what we are doing is the right thing.

Thus we begin to call on many different external authorities in our quest for certainty. Sometimes it is the Bible, or a particular tradition of biblical interpretation. At other times we call on the authority of history or "tradition," received wisdom, or the seminary professor who told us the "right" way to do some part of the liturgy. The need for certainty is as common among progressives as among traditionalists even though the two groups may emphasize different ways of being certain about different things. I think, however, that when we seek certainty we are either trying to cover up our insecurity or we want a way to escape the unsettling suspicion that we may be wrong while shutting out the possibility that those who disagree with us might have a point.

A classic example among Episcopalians is the way we conduct our liturgical disagreements. Christians have worshiped for two thousand years using a large variety of forms and ceremonies, so to think that there is only one theologically correct or objectively best way to do it is self-serving and lazy. Can we possibly be so arrogant as to imagine that the myriad forms and ceremonies that brought the challenge and comfort of the faith to generations after generations await the revelation of our liturgical preferences? Liturgical expression does matter; however, we do well to bear in mind that our liturgical preferences are not eternal verities. As I think of the overbearing and destructive manner in which so many clergy have imposed their preferences on congregations who thought otherwise, I wonder if, had they had a little more humility and a little less certainty, they might have rendered better service to the Lord.

That approach to the liturgy does highlight one of the ways clergy often try to get to certainty—by theologizing their preferences. Here is what I mean. Perhaps the finance committee is discussing the budget when the priest speaks up, wanting to spend money on a particular item that the budget can't accommodate. Instead of acknowledging that others might have a different point of view both on the merits of the item in question and on the wisdom of having an unbalanced budget, the priest says that doing it the way he wants is an example of "faith" or of "trusting the Spirit." So now to speak against either the project or the budget impact, you are demonstrating your lack of faith. See how easy that was?

Suddenly our preferred way of doing something is no longer merely one possible way of doing things among others. Now we can present it as the way God wants it to be done because we have thought up a theological-sounding or biblically-referenced way of talking about it. It's always an attempt to silence opponents by making them feel guilty for not agreeing with you, like attributing racism, sexism, or fascism to someone who disagrees with you. This is a game everybody can play, but the clergy, having often been taught the rules of the game as far back as seminary, are usually better at it than the laity and often get their way. Because we're so certain we're doing the right thing, we often imagine it doesn't matter how we do it.

In the 1980s, in conformity with the 1979 Book of Common Prayer, most Episcopal parishes replaced Morning Prayer with the Holy Eucharist as the principal service on the Lord's Day. One priest made the switch on his first Sunday as rector and held firm in the ensuing storm because he was certain he was doing the right thing. As a result he never got over feeling aggrieved and besieged, and his ministry and the parish were permanently weakened. Contrast this with the priest who took seven years to implement the change fully. Everyone knew where he was going, but not a single person left the parish.

As a rule, convincing ourselves that we are certain about something and that there is no doubt that we are right is a great help to getting what we want. Even if others don't like it and can give their own reasons for doing it another way, the zeal of our certainty will often brush aside objections, and we will get our way. If it means that others are so disgruntled by our high-handedness that they leave the church, the voice of our certainty will tell us that we fought the good fight and that the parish is better off without them. Even disastrous consequences, paradoxically, can convince us even more firmly that we did the right, though unpopular, thing, and that we have shared the sufferings of Christ. It is a good idea to keep these words of Oliver Cromwell before us when we encounter resistance to our ideas: "I beseech you, in the bowels of Christ, think it possible that you may be mistaken." Not only should we ask those with whom we disagree to think that they might be mistaken, we also need to ask ourselves frequently if we might be mistaken—if not about what we're doing, then at least about the way we're doing it.

Writing against the formation of a Christian party in postwar Britain, C. S. Lewis held that our desire for certainty exposes us to that temptation which the Devil spares none of us at any time—the temptation of claiming for our favourite opinions that kind and degree of certainty and authority which really belongs only to the Faith. The danger of mistaking our merely natural, though perhaps legitimate, enthusiasms for holy zeal, is always great... On those who add, "Thus says the Lord" to their merely human utterances descends the doom of a conscience which seems clearer and clearer the more it is loaded with sin. All this comes from pretending that God has spoken when He has not spoken.[2]

Despite the welcome Reformation assertion that the church can err, the higher the stakes, the more likely we are to take refuge in some unofficial doctrine of infallibility, that is, the idea that Christ preserves the church from certain kinds of error. Lord Acton said above, "There is no worse heresy than that the office sanctifies the holder of it." Individual holders of offices do sometimes believe that they have been immunized from error. It is certainly common today for people to believe that group processes lead to decisions that are always right. "We made the right decision each time," said a former member of the Commission on Ministry with regard to an applicant they had rejected, and then accepted on a subsequent application. "God has already chosen your new rector," search committees are sometimes assured, the idea being that following the process correctly will lead the committee ineluctably to God's choice. I've heard the same remark about the outcome of episcopal elections. I do not dispute that one chosen and ordained or instituted in accordance with the canons becomes a real bishop or priest or rector; I'm just not convinced that the decisions that brought one person to that point and kept another away can always be held to be free from error. Moreover, we should not assert that God has spoken in order to relieve ourselves of taking responsibility for our decisions. We may believe with Hymn 135 that God's providence is "manifest in gracious will, ever bringing good from ill," but to say that everything that happens is God's will is quite another assertion, even if we're speaking only of the church.

RESPONSIBLE OR IDEOLOGICAL?

I am not suggesting that we be paralyzed by doubting and second-guessing ourselves. Rather, we should heed the difference between what Dietrich Bonhoeffer called "responsible action" and "ideological action." For Bonhoeffer, ideology is whatever external principle we use to try to give ourselves certainty. It could be a political ideology, like National Socialism or Communism, or it could be a set of convictions about biblical interpretation or tradition. It could be liturgical principles or rules of thumb or anything at all that we use as a source of certainty outside ourselves and independent of the circumstances in which we find ourselves. It could also be a doctrine of infallibility.

One who acts responsibly, on the other hand, never has the security of knowing she is right; no one can know the ultimate rightness of their actions. They take into account all the circumstances and all the sources that might shed insight on the circumstances, but when they act, they cannot know God's judgment on their actions. In his book *Ethics* Bonhoeffer writes:

> Responsible action, in the consciousness of the human character of its decision, can never itself anticipate the judgment as to whether it is in conformity with its origin, its essence and its goal, but this judgment must be left entirely to God. All ideological action carries its own justification within itself from the outset in its guiding principles, but responsible action does not lay claim to knowledge of its own ultimate righteousness. ... The man who acts ideologically sees himself justified in his idea; the responsible man commits his action into the hands of God and lives by God's grace and favor.[3]

Bonhoeffer ultimately decided that in his circumstances responsible action meant taking part in a plot to kill Hitler, a decision that led to his imprisonment and execution. He is, therefore, hardly recommending an easy or unprincipled path. It requires an immense amount of humility and strength to act responsibly; it takes very little of either to act ideologically, which is the easy way out. If I have convinced myself that one way of reading the Bible or one way of performing the liturgy is correct in all times and places, then, without any difficult examination of myself or my circumstances, I am justified in doing whatever it takes to see that those who interpret the bible another way are silenced and those who prefer another liturgical style are disempowered. Responsible action does not give us the illusory security of thinking we're right. It requires of us the humility and strength to act in the absence of certainty. We examine ourselves, we analyze the circumstances, we solicit the views of those all around us; then we act without the comfort of "knowing" that we are right.

It becomes apparent that the attempting to attain certainty is yet one more way of maintaining one-way and abusive relationships. If my actions are ideological rather than responsible, then those who disagree with me can't really be my equals because I have the truth, and, by the definition provided by my certainty, they do not. I will either need to sequester myself in a sect of like-minded people, or I will need to make my truth prevail over the error of those who disagree. Perhaps I will feel justified in excluding those who do not share my definition of inclusivity. Perhaps I will feel justified in taking grossly uncharitable and unjust actions against a group of people by deluding myself that I hate only the sin, not the sinner. The use of principles that give us certainty as a justification for not respecting the dignity of every human being is found across the ideological spectrum. All can take refuge there, traditionalists and progressives, liberals and conservatives.

Over the course of this chapter the tight connection between humility and strength, at least in the way I am using the words, has, I hope, become clearer. Only those with accurate self-estimation and great inner strength can maintain two-way relationships when they are in leadership positions. Only the humble and strong can listen to the truth of how others experience them; weak leaders surround themselves with "yes-people" who will tell them only what they want to hear. Humble and strong leaders listen carefully to others' ideas and opinions; weak leaders act on their own preferences and fixed ideas. The former do not need outward signs of deference, while the latter require those they lead constantly to acknowledge their superiority; the former can take responsible actions and leave their ultimate judgment to God; the latter need to feel convinced that they are right, and that what they want always equals what is right.

You cannot be humble without being mentally and spiritually strong. It takes real inner strength to receive God's gift of seeing ourselves as others see us. Without humility, strength of character and self-confidence quickly become arrogance. In the next chapter we will examine the situations and circumstances that can cause the vision of ministry we saw so clearly at our ordination to be obscured. The circumstances of ministry are not always easy; there are personal and professional dynamics that can cause our perspective to change in ways that are not helpful to us and to those we serve.

End Notes:

1. Robert K. Greenleaf, *Servant Leadership: A Journey into the Nature of Legitimate Power and Greatness* (Mahwah, NJ: Paulist Press, 1977), 76. Emphasis Greenleaf's.
2. C. S. Lewis and Walter Hooper, eds, *God in the Dock: Essays on Theology and Ethics* (Grand Rapids, MI: Eerdmans, 1970), 198.
3. *Ethics*, translated by Neville Horton Smith (New York: Collier, 1986), 234.

CHAPTER THREE

THINGS THAT TWIST OUR VOCATIONS

The heart is devious above all else it is perverse—who can understand it? (Jer. 17:9)

I HAD NOT been working at the diocesan office for long when a rector who had been misusing parish money and was involved in a sexual relationship with a parishioner was deposed. An experienced priest colleague on the staff, who knew that I had had to apply several times to the Commission on Ministry before I was accepted for ordination, said to me, "However difficult you thought it was to get into this, it's harder to get out of this in one piece."

I have meditated on this observation a good deal over the years. My colleague spoke in the context of a case of ecclesiastical discipline, but I soon realized that his words could be applied much more widely. I have seen a good number of clergy who never had a disciplinary complaint lodged against them, but who reached retirement with significant levels of disappointment, anger, resentment, or remorse. There are those who have developed a slippery exterior nothing can stick to; they may have survived, but no one misses them when they're gone. And we've all known others who certainly appear to feel all right about themselves, but who are universally regarded as pompous blowhards, crazy or just plain impossible.

Clergy usually begin their ordained ministries with enthusiasm: "Look out church; here I come!" was how one friend described his feelings when he was ordained. An attitude adjustment is frequently required when new priests realize that the church is actually quite indifferent to their arrival on the scene. You may have been an important pillar of your congregation before ordination, served on powerful diocesan bodies, been a crackerjack seminarian, but after ordination you are a small fish among many. You may have tremendous gifts, but they aren't necessarily recognized and you may not get the opportunity to exercise them as you might have thought.

In introducing the disciplinary canons to groups of seminarians I have told them that only part of my purpose is to familiarize them with the procedures in the canons, especially as these are subject to periodic change. The larger aim is to help them set a course for their ministry that will both ensure that the disciplinary canons never need to be invoked, and, even more importantly, help them arrive at retirement, no matter what the trajectory of their ministry, feeling as good about their vocation and about the church as they felt at the moment of ordination. And no matter how they might feel about themselves, I also think it is important for them to gain and retain the respect of their colleagues and the laity with whom they minister so they aren't considered crazy or impossible. All of that is what I mean by "getting out in one piece."

This is not as easy as it may sound. There are plenty of situations and dynamics that can wither our vocations, twist them beyond recognition, or dash them in pieces. The purpose of this chapter is to examine closely a number of the things that prevent some clergy from getting out of this in one piece. They have trouble exercising leadership that is humble and strong, difficulty with establishing and maintaining two-way relationships in which people feel free to speak the truth to them. The focus of this chapter is how to recognize the symptoms of leadership that is disconnected, arrogant, weak, or ineffective.

WHAT ARE WE GETTING INTO?

We came to ordination with a great deal of enthusiasm and commitment. Recently ordained priests have invested years of their lives, a significant amount of money, and tremendous emotional and psychic energy preparing for ordination. We want it to work. Once we get there, however, things happen to most of us right away that can begin to eat away at our vocations. We can't avoid or ignore them, and how we respond early on can set us on a course that we follow for the rest of our ministries. I want to describe briefly some of the situations and dynamics that confront many of us when we are first ordained, and then examine some of the less productive ways of coping with what we face. I will concentrate on some of the unwelcome and negative aspects of our profession, the things clergy joke about or complain about with one another.

Of course this is only a part of our work. Watching and helping people come to faith, ministering to those in sickness and need, connecting with non-churchgoers in unexpected ways as we represent Christ and the church, glimpsing the mystery as we conduct the liturgy, sharing work and fellowship with people committed to Jesus and to one another, reconciling disagreements, and experiencing forgiveness from both sides—these and so much more are why we wanted to be ordained. But alongside these life-giving dimensions of our profession are the negative aspects, which I would term: money, living in a fishbowl, hard knocks, lack of support, and letdown. Most, if not all, clergy experience these to some degree, and it is useful for us to look at them because we frequently cope with these realities by adopting forms of behavior that make our leadership weak and arrogant. For example, our way of coping with the fishbowl aspect of parish ministry may be to adopt a defensive posture that makes it impossible for people to approach us with anything we do not want to hear. This will, of course, mean that we won't hear many things we *need* to hear. Or we might deal with inadequate compensation by misusing discretionary funds or by raising money outside the church to fund the things we'd like to get done. Not respecting boundaries around money is very dangerous and seldom turns out well.

So it is important for us to examine first the extent to which we have been affected by the downside of ordained ministry, and second, the appropriateness of the coping mechanisms we have adopted.

Money

Parish ministry has never been a remunerative profession. Certainly there are some high-paying positions in the church, but history indicates that the prayer of the lay leader—"You keep him humble, Lord; we'll keep him poor"—can still apply. The minimum compensation levels for the newly ordained are often quite low, and these days most of the newly ordained are carrying a hefty load of student debt. The financial burdens many clergy face are heavy and can be demoralizing, especially since most clergy are not by nature gifted financial managers. When the expenses of seminary have damaged a priest's credit rating, which can happen, there is an additional burden. Since the average age of ordinands is higher than it was forty years ago, new priests have existing obligations such as mortgages and education expenses for teenaged children that twenty-five-year-olds who went straight through college and seminary did not face. It is quite a strain to contribute toward your children's college expenses while you are paying off your student loans with a job that quite possibly pays considerably less than the one you had just before seminary.

Moreover, many congregations are also finding it harder to offer fulltime positions for the more experienced priest in charge of a congregation. The pastoral-sized congregation, typical of so many churches (average Sunday attendance of 75–100, a fulltime priest, and physical plant of moderate size) is under increasing strain. The minimum compensation package for a fulltime priest with ten or fifteen years of experience can reach or top $100,000 including pension and medical benefits. If the cost of the clergy and the payments to the judicatory (diocese, synod, conference, etc.) are more than half of operating income, it is likely that the congregation is under great financial pressure: perhaps pension and medical insurance payments are in arrears, and maintenance on the plant is being deferred. At the same time positions for curates and assistants have virtually disappeared except in the larger program and resource congregations. (This lack of assistants' positions has other consequences to which we will return.)

All of this means that new priests in their forties or fifties, whether male or female, with a load of student loans and perhaps a part-time position in the church, cannot be the primary breadwinner in the family. The spouse's job is no longer a supplement to the household; in many cases he or she is carrying most of the weight. This creates a new set of stresses and pressures that the culture of the church often has difficulty accommodating, since many parishes are still haunted by the ghost of an expectation of a "twofer" and assume the spouse will be a fulltime volunteer. Clergy families are usually devoted to the cleric's vocation and the family has no doubt made considerable sacrifices during the seminary years. However, the priest may need to look for a position in quite a restricted geographic area, depending on the spouse's employment, and the position he or she finds may not be the best fit. And, despite the devotion of the family to the priest's vocation, the subsequent moves the family makes may well need to be largely determined by the demands of the primary breadwinner's position.

Such financial pressures are not unique to clergy families, but there are other aspects of financial dealings in churches that increase the pressures on the cleric and the family. Most churches are not good at talking about money. A priest may feel guilty about making decisions for her family's well-being that are driven by financial considerations, while a lot of congregations are quite willing to allow the priest and his family to feel guilty while exploiting their willingness to put up with inadequate pay and a poorly maintained rectory.

Clergy often feel self-conscious and reluctant to talk about money both because it seems self-serving and because of the attitudes of vestries and parishioners—"You want us to give more so we can raise your salary and make repairs to the rectory. I wish I lived rent-free and made what you make!" (I have actually heard a churchwarden say that to her priest in a meeting.) Such a comment demonstrates that if budget need is the only basis on which the parish solicits pledges every year, people will make the connection that if they keep a budget line down, the need will be less. Congregations have balanced the budget on the backs of their priests for a long time. The priest's family can experience a high level of cognitive dissonance when the vestry members get into their BMWs and Escalades after firmly asserting yet again that they are supporting the church as much as they possibly can. It matters how clergy families figure out how to live with that dissonance.

Living in a Fishbowl

Many parishioners identify strongly with their pastor. This is a good thing, up to a point, of course. It's good for the parish: if people like the pastor, they will often be good evangelists for the parish, and certainly they'll be more likely to invite friends to church. It is good for the priest's morale, too. Most clergy like to be liked; it is easier to work with people who like you, and a little charm helps grease some wheels that would otherwise be hard to turn. We'll have more to say later on about the over-reliance on, and misuse of, charm and likeability; for now let's assume that the priest is likeable and charming in just the right degree.

One aspect of people's identification with you that can be unsettling is the extent to which people are watching you, and talking with others about what they see, and letting you know that they are watching and talking. A parishioner called a colleague of mine on his cell phone and asked him to open the church for a contractor. My friend said he couldn't do it. The parishioner said, "But I drove by just now and saw your car in the drive." My friend then had to explain that he had gone somewhere by public transportation so he wasn't at the rectory. The dynamic is like that of a very small town. Another priest was looking for an apartment in the small southern hamlet where he had been called and a parishioner warned him off one two-family house by saying, "Those people sometimes have their lights on as late as 11:00 p.m."

The parish is a fishbowl. I believe there is no other profession except politics in which the person's entire life is considered fair game. For most people it is sufficient to have their professional lives on display; doctors, lawyers, nurses, therapists, and teachers are all professionals whose effectiveness also depends on how they relate to their patients or clients or students. Clergy have all that, but in addition their child-rearing skills, their taste in home décor, and whom and when they entertain are just as much subject to scrutiny and analysis. Living in a fishbowl makes a jumble of the professional and the private. You probably won't be aware of strife in your doctor's family, but even if you are, it probably won't change your opinion of him as a doctor. It's often different with a priest. And, to a great extent, that's how it should be. The ordination services in the Episcopal Church all speak of the necessity of the bishop, priest or deacon to be a "wholesome example," and at the Celebration of a New Ministry the rubric suggests that the new minister's family also be presented to the congregation. This makes it clear that the role of the priest is not simply that of a professional hired to do a job. To some degree—a larger degree than some people can easily tolerate—the priest's personal and family life are part of the package; they can't and shouldn't be separate the way they are for others. Most people will give the priest and his family some privacy, but there will almost always be needy parishioners who will not.

Especially if you live in a rectory on the church grounds, it can also be difficult simply to make a mental separation between the time you're working and the time you're off. Parish ministry is not a nine-to-five job. It is necessary to create ways to feel that you are not working, but this can be difficult when you live over the store. If the sexton lives onsite people can go to him to let them into the church, but most places they'll knock on your door. All this takes some getting used to, if you can get used to it, and how you get used to it matters.

Hard Knocks

At a renewal of ordination vows on Holy Week the clergy were processing by date of ordination, those most recently ordained in the front. A friend with about fifteen years of service pointed out the fresh faces ahead of him, and said he was walking with those who "had been knocked around a little." If the church is the body of Christ, then, like Christ, the church is fully human and fully divine. We glimpse and touch the divine in the liturgy and in lives transformed by grace. We experience the fully human part of the church in the brutally indifferent way the machinery can operate and in the shameful way many Christians treat one another.

Clergy often do feel knocked around by the hierarchy and by the people they serve; the parish is not always a gentle place. Out of nowhere comes a fresh wave of resistance to something you thought was settled. Or you frequently find that you've been set up or blindsided or triangulated or thwarted. I have seen a change in the format of the Sunday bulletin cause a choir member to scream at the rector immediately after the service. Others throw you some major curve ball minutes before the service begins, just (it seems) to keep you off balance. Someone has complained about you to the diocesan office, and perhaps it was handled in a way that leaves you feeling exposed and unsupported. Even when things are going well, these dynamics are still difficult to deal with day after day.

Leaders who have long experience in the church can usually navigate these shoals without running aground, but an inexperienced priest can be badly injured in a fierce riptide. Some new clergy come to ordination with scant exposure to "normal" parish life because they did not grow up in a church, but had an adult conversion and went to seminary pretty quickly afterward. In my diocese the largest "resource parishes" produce the most candidates for holy orders, but these newly ordained priests will likely be serving in small places where the internal dynamics are completely different. Especially if it is a place that has experienced poor leadership and some kind of decline over a period of time, the negative dynamics are likely to be deeply rooted and difficult to deal with.

The traditional way of equipping priests with the necessary coping skills was to ordain people who had grown up and been active in the church; after ordination, they would serve a curacy for several years before they could have a parish of their own. Whether the majority of clergy ever actually fit this model, it is what our priestly formation process still seems to assume. Seminaries were intended to be only academic preparation for ministry in an age when writing two long sermons, one for Sunday morning and one for Sunday evening, was what the priest was expected to spend most of his time doing. Whatever practical preparation you had was assumed to come from your life in the church before seminary and from the rector whose curate you became afterward. So for good or ill, all the things "they never taught me in seminary" were, at least at the beginning, not intended to be taught there.

Curacies, where they exist, still come in two varieties: exemplary and cautionary. Most curates get a solid grounding in the many aspects of parish life by serving with a competent and kind rector. The rest can learn from their rectors only what not to do and how not to do it. Whatever the rector is like, it is always a valuable experience for an attentive assistant to do priestly work without the weight of responsibility for a congregation that the priest in charge must carry. If an assistantship is not possible, a mentor is a help, as are the programs for clergy in new cures, but these cannot replace daily interaction with a good supervising rector who can also run interference if things start to go awry. When a priest is put in charge of a congregation without that experience of being an assistant, there is increased danger that she will have some difficult rounds and may be knocked out of the ring.

In addition, it is not always recognized that a vocation to the priesthood is not necessarily the same as the ability to be in charge of a congregation. In the space of five years I saw two priests who had done solid work as assistants suffer breakdowns when they were put in charge of congregations. They could easily bear the weight of the specifically priestly task; that is what they wanted to do. However, they were not suited to being the executive director of a struggling not-for-profit with building problems, budget shortfalls, mediocre staff, unreasonable expectations on the part of the members, and a fair level of interpersonal conflict. Few people got ordained specifically in order to manage the institution, but the management of the buildings and budget is a vital part of being in charge of a congregation. It matters how we adjust to the realities of that task.

Lack of Support

In the mid-1980s a bishop took the priests in a certain area of the diocese to lunch. When some of them were asking him whether the diocesan office could assist with some things in the parishes they needed help with, the bishop said, "I trust you all to do a good job, but there's not much I can do for you. It's kind of sink or swim." In fact, it's often worse than that. If you swim, you don't get recognized or thanked; if you sink, you often do get blamed.

A study by Dean R. Hoge and Jacqueline E. Wenger entitled *Pastors in Transition: Why Clergy Leave Local Church Ministry* finds that "ministers are experiencing a lack of support and support systems, especially when they are coping with conflicts."[1] About half the clergy who had left the parish ministry did so because of conflict within the congregation (27%), conflict with denominational leaders (10%), or feelings of burnout or discouragement (12%). The three categories are related and shade into one another because a conflict within the congregation can become a conflict with denominational officials, while feeling unsupported is a major contributing factor to burnout.

The lack of support can be felt at all levels. In order to lead, one needs both the support of the group one is leading and challenges from that group that test the vision. While many clergy are appropriately supported and challenged by the leadership and membership of their congregations, there is frequently a lack of appropriate support and a surfeit of challenges to the leader. Furthermore, clergy may hope to find supportive relationships with their colleagues, but such relationships may be hard to come by. Clergy can be competitive in a system that tends to encourage them not to admit to weaknesses. "The pope is in perfect health until he dies," as the saying goes. It can be difficult to ask for help until everything has blown up.

And if the parish is a fishbowl, so is the profession. Clergy must choose their confidantes carefully; a "clerical secret," so the joke runs, means that you tell only one person at a time. Even if confidentiality is maintained, one thinks twice before being vulnerable with a colleague who may one day be a superior. Clergy usually have easy, comfortable and helpful collegial relationships with one another, but if there are two colleagues with whom you can be truly open, you are fortunate.

The lack of support clergy frequently feel from the judicatory depends only to some extent, I believe, on the personalities of the individual bishops and staff members involved. The disconnect the congregations feel between themselves and the diocesan office is both systemic and very difficult to address.

Some years back a new diocesan staff member who was to work with congregations on their building problems came to me after he'd made several site visits and said, "There is a lot of resentment of the diocesan office out there." I told him that the relationships between the diocesan offices and the several parishes were long and convoluted, often characterized by poor communication and misunderstandings. Because the nuances of these stories are difficult to remember, I said, "The way the parishes tend to remember the stories is, 'It was the diocese's fault.'" Of course parishes are often happy to take advantage of diocesan programs and resources, but no matter how well-served a parish may feel by one part of the diocesan structure, there will usually be resistance and resentment in other areas. The fact remains that clergy often feel that the diocesan structure is not their best or most reliable source of support, and all too often that judgment can be sustained by a hundred proofs.

Letdown

In my observation, a feeling of letdown is one response to the vicissitudes of the ministry. Money, lack of privacy and getting knocked around can be contributing factors, but underneath there can be the realization that this kind of service is just not what we expected or really want. Whatever it was you thought the priesthood would be, the reality of its daily practice simply isn't it. A priest who comes to feel this way doesn't necessarily leave the ministry, yet one can sense a distaste and disappointment in how some clergy speak of their work.

So many parts of the life of the institution are a real disappointment, and not everyone has the stomach to be in the engine room. The letdown can be a fundamental disenchantment with the church. Vicious politics, competitiveness, complacency, lives that have not been transformed even after a lifetime of Christian observance—from time to time in some way these realities will call into question at least for some of us what we are doing and why we're doing it. A priest nearing retirement after more than thirty-five years of effective parish work said to a younger colleague, "When I retire, I won't go near another [expletive] Episcopal church!"

Of course these negative aspects are not the whole story, but they may be part of the story. It is not helpful either to deny them or to be overwhelmed by them. If you find that this is not for you, it isn't necessary to conclude that the vocation was erroneously discerned. Every job—including one you love—comes with some duties that you probably don't love and this is especially true of a parish priest. Clergy rarely have the luxury of being specialists; they must be generalists, willing and able to tend adequately to the liturgical, educational, formational, pastoral, programmatic, financial, physical, and administrative parts of the life of the congregation. They need to have a vision or a sense of the direction in which the parish can move and manage difficult relationships successfully. And they must help set up tables and chairs and perhaps fire up the boiler. When a friend told the vestry of his plans to take early retirement, one of the wardens blurted out, "Oh no. Now we'll have to hire a sexton!"

Those who go on after their first cure have figured out ways to reorder their finances, to live in a fishbowl, to stand up after being knocked flat, to address their need for support, and to live with the disappointing and frustrating realities of the institution. Some become humble and strong, increasing daily in inner fortitude and a realistic sense of themselves and others. Others take different courses. We will spend the rest of this chapter looking at some of the inappropriate coping mechanisms leaders can adopt. These mechanisms are injurious, even toxic, to your vocation, and they don't do any favors for the people and institutions you serve.

UNFAIRNESS AND THE EROSION OF MORALE

It is important to avoid being in a situation where the terms of employment are simply not fair. I know of rectors who have told prospective curates that they can have either the minimum salary or their pension assessments paid, or that they must choose between medical insurance and the pension. Of course this is completely against the canons, but I don't believe there is anyone with less power in the church than a newly-ordained assistant. Or in some-one's first solo assignment in a small and struggling parish, the vestry may say that there isn't enough money to reimburse professional expenses like business travel, or want to pay less than the minimum compensation, or expect a half-time compensation package to equal fulltime work. Especially if you are new and enthusiastic, your de-sire to do the work will be so great that you may well agree to these terms. Things will be fine for awhile: you'll have fun doing the work, you'll learn all kinds of things, and you won't care about not getting reimbursed for your travel. That lasts for about a year.

Then, almost as if there is an automatic timer in your spirit, the unfairness of it will start to eat at you. You'll see colleagues in jobs that look less stressful who get the normal benefits and expense reimbursements. You'll have an unexpected auto repair bill that would have been a whole lot easier to pay if you'd been getting your business travel reimbursed. You'll go to a retirement planning workshop and start to feel a little sour about the pension assessments that aren't being paid for your work. It'll be difficult to approach the vestry about it. If you're the curate, you can't. If you're the priest who agreed not to be reimbursed for travel, you'll probably not want to bring it up because, after all, you agreed to it. And the vestry is happy not to have that expense.

What do you do? If you're the curate, and your pension assess-ments are not being paid, I can imagine only that you're in a seri-ously one-way relationship with your rector. He will not want to hear about fairness. I would counsel you, if possible, to go to the diocesan administrator or the bishop and see if there's a way to rectify the situation. The reality is that the diocesan office may be unwilling or unable to help, or there may not be a way it can help without endangering your position. If that is the case, you'll need to wait until you get another position. Then you can try to get those arrearages paid within the time limits set by the Pension Fund so you don't lose the years of credited service. Maybe there's a way to see that no future curate is treated that way, but maybe not.

If you're in that parish that isn't reimbursing your travel, or that isn't paying you according to your diocese's minimum compensa-tion levels, here is something else that may happen. Maybe you have a discretionary fund with a separate account, and you're the only signatory. Maybe your honoraria for weddings and funerals are directed to that fund as a condition of your employment so they are not taxable income to you. Maybe people are making contributions to the fund because they like you and may even feel a little guilty for exploiting you. It might occur to you that what the vestry is withholding on one end, you might give yourself from that fund, and so you start paying your car repair bills from your discretionary fund. You probably sense that this is not right, but, as you tell yourself, what the parish is doing isn't right either. It is the health of your vocation that is at stake here. We'll talk later about what happens inside you when you don't respect the boundaries around money and sex; the effects are pernicious even if nothing comes out publicly about it.

SERVING A PARISH YOU WOULDN'T ATTEND

At a clergy day soon after I was ordained, I wondered aloud at my table, "How many people here are serving a parish they wouldn't attend if it didn't employ them?" It was clear from the reaction that a number of them felt themselves in that situation and it isn't a pleasant place to be. The more our leadership is characterized by humility and strength, the easier it will be for us to connect to a parish. However, when the priest can't feel some kind of genuine connection with the parish and its people, it's difficult to muster an enthusiastic vision for what can happen there. Relationships are more difficult to manage in that situation because people will sense your lack of connection, and it will be hard for you to be much of an evangelist.

Maybe you even feel a bit ashamed of the parish because of an ugly plant, or the culture or class of the members, or just because it's a small, out-of-the-way place. Merely lacking a connection with the place makes effective ministry harder and might motivate you to find a better fit, but feeling ashamed of the place is a little more dangerous. The coping mechanisms you might adopt in that circumstance might be injurious, especially if you can't leave. These are the situations in which I have seen people become pompous or crazy. It appears that becoming self-important or really out of touch are possible ways of compensating for being in a place we wish we could get out of.

GETTING STUCK

Getting stuck is what happens when you stay too long in a place you're ashamed of or one you can't connect to. It's also what can happen if you stay too long in a place you really have loved but can no longer effectively serve.

The common wisdom now favors a stay of about seven years in one parish. Long pastorates are often seen as a problem, as indeed many are. Some clergy can serve thirty-five years in the same parish without ever losing their creative and effective touch, but this is the exception. A period of between five to ten years will allow an energetic leader to articulate and implement a shared vision, which might result in a capital campaign or real renewal and growth in the educational or outreach ministry of the parish. After that, it may be difficult to stay fresh. You may not be able to move the vision forward in that place. If attendance grew at a gratifying pace for some years, it may level off or drop. What worked at first may no longer work as well as it once did. The annual cycle stagnates, with the same hymns in the same places on the major days; at least that's what happened to me as a church organist thirty years ago.

Over time we can also lose the ability to challenge the parish culture because we have become part of it. Perhaps there is more talk about great things that happened in the past than about great things to work toward in the future. Or maybe you tried to move several times, but never got the job you were seeking. If your parish is in the doldrums, as can happen in these situations, then it can become harder to move because the record doesn't look that good. Depression, alcohol abuse, isolation, inattention to basic parish duties—all these are possible when one feels stuck. There can also be a level of self-delusion as we try to convince ourselves that the situation is not what it is, and that we don't feel what we are feeling. The downward spiral continues. One priest said to me, "I don't want to leave while the parish is not doing well. That's why I'm still here." These can be very sad situations.

I've seen three ways that the lay leadership and the congregation respond when the priest is stuck. All three can be in evidence in the same parish. Some may be devoted to the priest and express that devotion by covering up for him, explaining away problems, and generally enabling a bad situation to continue. Or, if the person is close enough to retirement—however that may be defined—and the situation isn't totally out of control, there may be a tacit agreement to let it go on while working to mitigate any negative effects. Or the situation goes out of control and the judicatory may get involved. In general the canonical tools the judicatory has to intervene in parish affairs are not precision instruments; they are blunt, and one can expect a fair amount of collateral damage.

DEFENSIVENESS

Defensiveness is probably everyone's most common response to any kind of criticism, and when subordinates or parishioners try to tell us their truth, we usually take it as criticism and respond defensively. It is a response intended to block negative information or distressing feelings so we can maintain our self-image. For lots of leaders the negative information that needs to be blocked is people's criticisms of us. We feel attacked, judged, inadequate, or unpopular. Then our first impulse is to try to divert the focus, intimidate the person offering the criticism, or distort reality by creating a self-image that cannot be touched by others' negative perceptions.

If we feel responsible for a pledge campaign that hasn't gone very well, any discussion of the budget will be threatening to us. If we're already feeling anxious, the suggestion by a lay leader that a particular budget line be reduced may easily set us off because we are primed to see almost any comment as a criticism of our performance that we ourselves are not happy with.

If several aspects of parish life aren't going particularly well, discussions of any of them will trigger our defenses. If we're approached by strong individuals, we'll develop tactics for heading off conversations that we think might address things we don't want to talk about. With a certain tone of voice or flash of the eyes we'll be able to silence weaker people. If the situation worsens, we'll find a way of looking at it that gets us off the hook but significantly differs from the reality others perceive. The more defensiveness we show, the worse our relationships will become; the worse our relationships, the less successful the life of the parish will be, and the greater the need for more defensiveness. The downward spiral continues.

Defensiveness is possible in any relationship in which we see ourselves as some kind of victim. Perhaps we're defensive because we suspect that we're not doing as good a job as we could be or need to be doing. Defensiveness is always a response to a perceived attack. Whether it is or not, defensiveness is an unhelpful response that poisons relationships. It works in the short term by shielding us from negative input and anxious feelings. Discounting any merit in the perceived criticism, our anxiety becomes an anger we feel is justifiable. A defensive subordinate who is competent can often be brought to be more trusting by a patient supervisor, but it is impossible to have a satisfactory working relationship with a defensive superior. Defensive clergy hurt and weaken their parishes.

Defensiveness manifests itself in two ways, and one is the tendency to personalize conflict. If someone disagrees with us, we view it as an attack, not a disagreement. Once we've characterized the disagreement or criticism as a personal attack, then it's not necessary to discuss the merits of the case and see if we can come to some agreement. We tell ourselves we are justified in being angry at the person, and justified in questioning the person's motives and her good faith. All this tends to the conclusion that someone who disagrees with me is not only wrong, but he is also a bad person. Not very far down this road comes the idea that because he is bad, it is all right for me to do whatever is necessary either to silence or get rid of him.

You can suspect that you're personalizing conflict when you hear yourself say, "If Joe and Mary would just go away, everything would be fine." That's almost sure to be a misleading simplification of the situation.

Years ago I was bringing the Sunday school in to join the main service with another adult who was helping that week. One spirited little boy was acting up as usual, and my helper responded very angrily. When I remonstrated, she said, "He's doing that just to get at me." I said, "I don't think he really knows who you are, and he acts that way all the time." Of course the boy has grown into a very nice adult, as most difficult children do. My friend, alas, has had a rockier row. It's often nothing personal, and, whether it is nor not, it seems best to let it go.

Although those who personalize conflict tend to think they can solve things by getting rid of the person they've identified as the problem; in fact most problems are either systemic or involve more than one person, such as a triangle. It will almost certainly not be fixed by making one person go away.

This is an especially tough one to accept because if the problem is systemic, it means I'm probably involved in it. In fact, if I'm the leader, the principal responsibility for the problem is more likely to be mine than anyone else's. Of course it's easier to blame one person, although that will do nothing to make the system healthier. Probably another scapegoat will be needed before too long, yet many parish clergy and plenty of supervisors still think that getting rid of one individual they find troublesome will make everything all right. Resist the temptation to imagine that it will. Scapegoating is really never an effective management technique.

AVOIDING RESPONSIBILITY

One way to deal with the criticism and pressure of ministry is to avoid taking responsibility for anything. We probably all know clergy who seem to have developed a Teflon coating; nothing sticks to them. The people I've known who have developed this non-stick surface are usually pleased with this adaptation to the stresses of ministry. They don't need to engage with people or situations. They attend many meetings but never leave with anything to do except attend the next meeting. They get others to take the disagreeable actions they don't want to have attributed to them.

People who avoid responsibility seem to think it's a way of avoiding any difficulties. If nothing can be pinned on me, then nothing that goes wrong can be my fault. I'll jump in and take credit for what has gone well, but I'm nimble enough that if a good situation I've taken credit for starts to turn bad, I'll be sure my fingerprints aren't on it by the time it goes south. Such people usually seem to think that avoiding responsibility will preserve their popularity: if people can't blame me for anything, then they will have a positive opinion of me. Of course it doesn't work that way. If you're making sure no bad thing can be traced to you, it means you're always leaving others holding the bag. Avoiding responsibility always means that you'll reflexively throw your colleagues, subordinates, or anyone else under the bus.

Teflon people want a position in which they don't exactly report to anyone else, and certainly nobody reports to them. If you've worked with such people, you know that the only thing worse than having them in a peripheral position is having them in a position of real responsibility. As co-workers they will annoy you by trying to pin all the blame on you; if they're actually in charge of something, things get worse. They will be concerned only about themselves and how they look, and because they are not willing to learn how to exercise responsibility daily, in a measured way, they'll tend to let bad situations develop and fester. Furthermore, those who avoid responsibility are the last ones who want it brought to their attention, so they will always maintain one-way relationships.

The Problem with Charm, Good Looks, and Youth

If you don't come to ordination with a winning personality, it helps to develop one. When you need to recruit teachers, when you're trying to make a change, when you're refereeing a squabble, a little charm is useful. As for your appearance, because people do identify with their pastor, you have a duty to look as well as you can. But charm is not a substitute for substance; clergy who rely too much on youth and looks have a bigger-than-normal midlife adjustment awaiting them.

"Your wife will be in my prayers," said a charming, witty, and urbane priest to the senior warden after a vestry meeting. The woman was having critical surgery the next day in a hospital less than a block from the church. His pious remark was the priest's way of saying that he had no intention of visiting her in the hospital, and he didn't. The priest left that parish about a year later just before the vestry was going to vote to dissolve the pastoral relationship. When it became apparent that he was simply unwilling to discharge his responsibilities, his charm and wit were coins of small value.

Looks, charm and (relative) youth can perhaps help doors open more easily, but when the doors open, people need to see a real person who sincerely cares and who works hard.

Charisma

Charisma is that force of personality which impresses and captivates those around you. During the "return to religion" of the postwar period, "charisma" enjoyed as great a vogue as "relevance." Charisma is like curly hair: either you have it or you don't. It's not something you can develop. Lots of leaders have felt inadequate because they know they aren't charismatic, but in my experience charisma is more a liability in a leader than an asset. That is because the purpose of leadership is to focus attention on the community or organization, and on the possibilities and challenges it faces. If the leader is charismatic, the focus will inevitably be on the leader, not on the organization and its environment.

The opposite of "charismatic" is not "boring," but "transparent." A charismatic leader is always visible, always drawing attention to herself. When you look at her, you see someone who takes up a lot of space in the room and you are constantly aware of her presence. Those who like the charismatic leader will talk about how much they like the way he does the liturgy. A leader who is humble and strong, on the other hand, is present but less visible, less in evidence. When you look at her, you'll see someone you probably like, but you may also see through her to the God she is trying to present. People in that congregation will talk more about the liturgy itself and its effect on them than about the person conducting it.

Both charismatic leaders and humble, strong leaders are attractive figures to whom people respond. A charismatic leader will be able to motivate people to help with the institution because of their admiration for him. People will respond equally to the authenticity of a leader who is humble and strong, but she will concentrate on transferring their focus of devotion to the parish and to the work. The humble and strong leader will feel she has missed the mark if people's devotion remains directed at her.

"LONE RANGERS"

It is the nature of the church to gather. We gather locally every week, and periodically in larger groups. Churches are by nature connectional organizations, even if the polity of the denomination is congregational. Non-denominational churches have also developed these kinds of bonds. It is simply the nature of the church to gather.

Some clergy are "lone rangers," however, and it almost always turns out to be a problem. Within a few years of being on the diocesan staff, for example, I had met or spoken to all the parish clergy with the exception of three. For different reasons each of these three never came to convention, the priests' conference, or to any other gathering. In one case the priest had been beaten down so hard by a particularly complicated series of encounters with the machinery that he had simply gone to ground and was not about to put his head up in a way that would invite further kicks.

In the other two cases an energetic priest had taken on a congregation that needed to be rebuilt and both were succeeding in terms of attendance, though somewhat less than you'd expect in terms of money. There were some snags—late parochial reports, difficulties getting the assessment payments, and the troublesome fact that neither priest came to any diocesan gatherings and neither did anyone from their parishes. The two situations both ended badly, one somewhat more spectacularly than the other. The income of one of the parishes had grown to the point that certified financial statements were required instead of the more informal audit procedure used by smaller congregations. The rector and treasurer fought fiercely not to have a CPA audit, citing the cost, and not too long afterward, the priest, still married, was found to be in a sexual relationship with a parishioner. As that was being dealt with, the truth began to come out about the money. With the treasurer's connivance, quite a bit of parish money had been flowing through a personal account and was unaccounted for. The other priest had not misused money; he had just constantly demanded more than the parish could really pay. And, of course, he was also having an extramarital affair.

This taught me that numbers really are not the whole story and that why we do what we do is as important as how we do it.

I realized that in each case the priest was doing an apparently successful job but for the wrong reasons, and these wrong reasons ended up sabotaging their work. If our primary motivation is our own ego gratification rather than the glory of God and the health of the church, there will be serious distortions in our vocation. Both clergy kept to their parishes because that was the main source of gratification. They saw no point in participating in other gatherings, because there was no payoff to be had there.

There might be additional reasons that clergy end up being lone rangers. Feeling so beaten down by the system that you dare not and cannot bear to show your face, and creating a parish that gives you all the adulation you need—these are the causes I've seen. Whatever the cause, the fact remains that it is always a danger signal if a leader in an organization that is all about gathering avoids gatherings.

SEX AND MONEY

Leo Tolstoy was wrong in his opening paragraph of *Anna Karenina*. Happy families may be all alike, but so are unhappy people and unhappy families. The prophet Jeremiah was right: the human heart is truly impossible to understand. Over and over, generation after generation, people make the same relatively small number of career-ending blunders and ruinous mistakes. An editorial in *The New York Times* about former senator from Alaska, Ted Stevens, began, "One of life's enduring mysteries is why powerful people risk substantial reputations and careers for relatively insubstantial sums of money. Perhaps the answer is power itself and the sense of entitlement and invulnerability it confers."[2] Our failure to respect boundaries around money and sex is probably the most common way we do ourselves in. Stories about sex are more memorable, but the misuse of money is more common and more dangerous to the health of our vocations than sexual escapades.

One reason is that money is a bigger part of our lives than our libido. Money takes more of our attention; we need to think of it a great deal, both in our professional and in our personal lives.

If those past adolescence were able to track how much mental space and energy are taken up by their anxieties, plans, and hopes around the getting and spending of money, and how much by sexual memories or fantasies, the former would just about always win. Another reason is that we can't swear off money just as we can't swear off food. (That is why obesity is a bigger problem than alcoholism.) It is easier for many of us to go cold turkey in giving something up than it is for us to use in moderation something pleasurable. How much more difficult would it be for alcoholics if we "needed" two drinks a day the way we need a certain number of calories or a certain amount of money?

Another reason money is frequently misused, especially in the church, is that often clergy are not held to account for their use of money. Many clerics have discretionary accounts on which they are the only signatory, and on which they never report. The Rev. Canon William Geisler, former Controller Emeritus of the Diocese of California, tells clergy gatherings that "sunshine kills germs." If you have money that you know no one will ever ask you to report on, you are living in a dark and dank atmosphere in which germs will multiply. Even if you are familiar with the rules around the use of discretionary funds, it remains the case that if we know that the part of the parish's money that is in our discretionary fund will never be checked or audited, we will be much more likely to blur the boundaries and give ourselves permission to use it for personal expenses.

It doesn't take much to set up a system that keeps us accountable for the use of money, however. Do not have a separate account for the discretionary fund, but keep it with other parish money, and ask the treasurer for reimbursements or advances as needed.

KEEPING SECRETS

Confidentiality is different from secrecy. The ability to keep confidences is always good but doing something that must be kept a secret is almost always bad. Confidentiality is simply limiting sensitive information about someone else to the appropriate number of people; sometimes the appropriate number is just you. The contents of a confession are never to be discussed with anyone else. More often confidential information is known to a number of people. A search committee has a good deal of information that is not to be shared outside the committee. The information isn't secret; there's nothing illegal or immoral being covered up. It's just that the contents of interviews and the discussion that brings a committee to a recommendation are not for public consumption.

A secret is something that would cause a real problem if it were to come to light. There will almost certainly be something in the life of each of us that would cause us difficulties if it were to become known, especially in our zero-tolerance, "gotcha" culture. We've all sent e-mails that have been forwarded to the wrong person; we've all said things that would sound pretty terrible if quoted out of context. If anyone could recall what we may have said during a game of "Never Have I Ever," the drinking game that involves revealing personal information, it might be a bit embarrassing. There is almost certain to be something in our past that we'd prefer not to bring up now. There is likely to be something in our current life that we'd rather not have talked about.

There is always going to be some discrepancy between the life we show to others and what really is going on. The problem lies with those things going on right now that would jeopardize our reputations or our careers if they came out, matters most likely to do with drink, money, or sex—not only because they're so common, but because they're the things that get people's attention. Running your office like Attila the Hun or overspending the endowment does more damage to the institution and the lives of your staff, but it is not going to get you into the same amount of trouble as a drunk driving arrest, an extramarital affair, or paying for your mother's vacation from your discretionary fund. If you are keeping dangerous secrets like these, you may or may not have thought about the potential consequences. If the secret is alcohol use, you may not be aware of how far you are down the road. If it's a sexual affair or misuse of funds, you probably have thought about what might happen, and you've decided to go ahead anyway. There are probably very painful reasons why you've done that. And it's difficult to get off that horse once it starts trotting.

If your life really is an open book, be grateful. I doubt that many clergy who have secrets are happy about it.

EXPECTATIONS AND ENTITLEMENT

One way we keep ourselves from a healthy humility is by laying expectations on others and by feeling entitled to certain treatment or certain perks. There are relationships where expectations are called for; for example, employers certainly need to tell volunteers and paid staff what the job is and how they'd like it done. Here again, though, the expectations need to run both directions. If employees are expected to perform a particular job, employers should be expected to support and back up their employees and to deal fairly and transparently with them, and there must be some way of calling the employer as well as the employee to account. If only the subordinate has to meet expectations, then we're still in a one-way relationship that lacks accountability.

In both professional and personal relationships, I think we should be reluctant to think in terms of expectations because the word includes a threat that is at least implied, if not explicit. The implication is that if my expectations of you are not realized to my satisfaction, there will be some kind of sanction— at minimum some kind of discussion about your failure to meet my expectations, and perhaps even a rupture in the relationship. This is not how adults should treat one another. If you do want to think in terms of expectations in your relationships in the workplace or in the parish, make sure that the expectations the other person has of you can also be measured and discussed. On the whole I think it's better to have high hopes and no expectations of others.

That may sound flippant, but it's not. In my observation and experience people will almost always respond with loyalty, devotion, and the best work they can possibly do when they feel that the leadership of the unit or organization is leading them somewhere good. They need to know that their supervisor is someone who is approachable, someone who notices good work and expresses appreciation for it, someone who is ready to listen to suggestions and ideas, and most importantly, someone who has their back and will go to bat for them, not triangulate them or throw them under the bus. If you're that kind of leader, you have probably already found that when people know that they can trust their superiors, it's fairly easy for anyone in the organization to talk anytime about anything at all that could be going better. Anxiety-producing discussions of expectations are superseded by constant mutual evaluation, camaraderie, and real teamwork.

Furthermore, it is not difficult for one-way expectations to morph into feelings of entitlement, which are always dangerous. If you come to feel that you must be deferred to in a particular way, or that you are entitled to something others are not, you are probably already deep into one-way relationships with others. In fact, feelings of entitlement are always a sign of one-way relationships. The sense of entitlement is always about what someone else owes me; I don't think that feeling entitled to something ever has to do with my responsibilities and my obligations in a relationship of mutual accountability.

EXITING BADLY

Most clergy serve their congregations faithfully and retire gracefully, receiving the thanks of a grateful community and saying goodbye and allowing others to say goodbye in a healthy way. Some, however, make missteps at this point that tarnish the memory of their service and often reveal the weaknesses latent in their ministry.

Money is usually part of the problem here. It appears that when we are taking our last pass at the trough, some of us want to grab as much as we can. One priest who felt he had been treated badly loaded up his car with every roll of toilet paper and paper towels from the parish house when he left. He also decided that the doorknobs throughout the Victorian rectory were his, and he "sold" them to the interim priest-in-charge for fifty dollars.

One such grab that seems to be more and more common is a three- or six-month "sabbatical" at the end of one's tenure. It's fine if a parish or diocese wants to pay the departing person for some extra period, but that is not a sabbatical. Let's keep our language clear.

For example, what somebody pays you for the use of your space is rent, not a "space use donation." Nor is extra vacation at the end of your tenure a sabbatical; a sabbatical means that you are coming back refreshed for further service. Let's call it what it is—"terminal leave," or "We're going to pay her for six more months."

A lay leader from one New York parish asked me, "Is it true that we are supposed to buy the priest an apartment when he retires?" I told my caller that his parish had done quite enough by paying the pension assessment. In another case, after spending the endowment to zero so there was no insurance on the building, payroll could often not be made, and the arrival of the utility bill precipitated a monthly crisis, a retiring rector told the chair of the finance committee that, unless he was permitted to lease the rectory apartment for much less than market rent, it would be a "deal-breaker." "What are you going to do?" she replied, "Stay?"

Housing may be a particular issue in major urban centers, but retirement purses cause problems everywhere. The IRS has a straightforward rule about when retirement purses are income. If the donors get a charitable deduction, the gift is considered income to the cleric. If people make personal gifts to the priest, there is no deductible gift and there's no taxable income. I have seen priests furious that they have to pay taxes on a six-figure retirement gift. A greedy departure really seems out of character with an effective ministry. I can think of two housing schemes that were floated by two very good priests. One came about; the other didn't, but both left a bad taste in people's mouths and colored their memories of the priests' entire ministry.

If fear of not having enough money in retirement was the motive in these examples, unwillingness to let go can cause other problems. A long-serving priest asked for several months beyond the mandatory retirement age in order to complete a project that had been going on for years. Of course it was not brought to conclusion within that time. The couple then delayed vacating the rectory for nearly a year even though they already owned the house they were planning to retire to. Another retiree who settled too close to the parish he had served for over thirty years took to writing long e-mails to the bishop's office to complain about the priest who followed him. Someone else fought long and hard to figure out a way he could appoint his successor.

In none of these situations could the priests' leadership have been characterized as humble and strong. In every instance the priest had maintained the outward appearance that all was well, while the reality was otherwise. It isn't surprising that priests whose ministry has been ineffective or destructive will exit gracelessly. The messy departure is what usually brings attention to the situation the priest was trying to cover up, so that how the ministry ended was consistent with how it was conducted all along.

RATIONALIZATIONS

Most of us end up making the kinds of mistakes outlined in this chapter only because we have figured out how to rationalize them to ourselves. Rationalizations are an aspect of the distortion of reality that is part of the defensive response. They are an important tool in keeping the truth at bay, and they are the principal way we make sure we don't see ourselves as others see us. The less grounded we are in relationships that are mutually accountable, the greater and more elaborate our collection of rationalizations will be. And no one will be in a position to tell us what we're doing. We will have seen to that.

There was an extremely sad case of a priest who had gotten stuck for a very long time in a parish. He had always been self-absorbed and eccentric, but in earlier years he had worked hard and his enthusiasm had had positive results. However, a situation that lacked basic fairness and caused him to lose several years with the Pension Fund, then consequent issues with misuse of funds, alcohol, poor adaptation to living in the parish fishbowl, lone rangerism, over-reliance on charm, personalizing conflict, feelings of entitlement—it was all there. And it was all perfectly rationalized. His critics were "bad people"; he didn't have an alcohol problem; he had a special arrangement with the diocesan office that meant his parish didn't have to follow the rules that applied to everyone else; everyone liked him and thought highly of him. Conversations with him were painful because he honestly cosidered himself one of the most senior respected priests of the diocese. By the last ten years of his ministry it was clear that he was beyond eccentricity and that an intervention was needed. No one took action, however, and by the end of his ministry (which ended very badly, needless to say) the distortions were so great that his reality barely intersected with the one the rest of us more or less share.

His was an extreme case, but it was different only in degree, not in kind, from others that you can probably think of. That priest's defense mechnanisms had reached such a technically advanced state that all unwelcome content was translated into the language of his rationalizations before it was allowed to enter his consciousness. Most of us are not quite that adept at rationalizations, but I have seen clergy feel justified in demanding a salary far larger than anyone in a similar situation. I've seen charismatic clergy bring the institutions they led to the brink of collapse and then retire, apparently satisfied with themselves. In one situation, a priest solicited a large mailing list of non-parishioners for donations for a particular program, deposited in a personal account the tens of thousands of dollars that people gave annually with checks made to the church, and used the money for the expenses of his extramarital affair. He said that this was how the priest he had first worked for had told him to handle his discretionary funds. (Who knows? That might be true.) And he told me he had thought long and hard about why I as the controller of the diocese should have a problem with his actions before it finally occurred to him that all I was after was the diocesan assessment on that money

Lack of accountability is a slippery slope. Once we start down it is difficult to stop, in part because we won't let anyone tell us we're sliding down There is no substitute for wanting to be accountable and for creating intentions and habits that help to remind us that we want to be accountable and to keep us accountable. To that we now turn.

End Notes:

1. Dean R. Hoge and Jacqueline E. Wenger, eds., *Pastors in Transition: Why Clergy Leave Local Church Ministry* (Grand Rapids: Eerdmans, 2005), 198.
2. "End of the Road for Ted Stevens," *The New York Times,* October 29, 2008.

CHAPTER FOUR

WAYS TO STAY ON TRACK: ELEVEN SUGGESTIONS

Who then is the faithful and wise servant, whom his master has set over his household, to give them their food at the proper time? (Matt. 24:45)

NOWADAYS THE CHURCH does not provide much institutional accountability and lacks reliable ways of training and forming people to be effective leaders, as the military trains and forms its officer corps or even as corporations train their executives. The structure that used to exist to prepare clergy to be good rectors or head pastors was serving as an ordained assistant in a parish. As parish churches decrease in size, however, those assistantships are largely gone. Therefore people are deployed in various states of readiness to be a leader into positions in which they are largely accountable to no one; these are "solo" positions. Mentorships and programs like Fresh Start in the Episcopal Church, which brings together clergy in new cures once a month for two years, are helpful; they are not, however, the same as working under the direct supervision of a kind and competent senior minister who can direct, counsel, guide, warn, and become a positive example that will endure throughout the curate's ministry.

Assistantships, of course, were never foolproof ways of forming good priests. However, if recently ordained people are taking solo positions in which they will not be supervised and held accountable in kind and constructive ways, there is an even greater possibility that bad habits will develop. How will I manage my time? How many hours of work are enough, and what are the most effective ways of spending them? How do I keep a suggestion to the Altar Guild from blowing up into a mess? Should baptisms be conducted the way my seminary professor preferred, or do I follow the parish custom? How can I recruit a chair for the Stewardship Committee, and how will we plan the pledge drive? What can I say about other people's giving, when I'm so stretched with seminary debt that I'm giving very little to the parish? How do I deal with those who are unhappy with some small change I have introduced? What is it desirable and feasible to think we can accomplish within the next year? How do I deal with the parts of this job that I don't particularly like and those I don't feel I'm good at?

Hundreds of questions like these come at the newly ordained all at once. Left to our own devices, we may come up with answers that are a little self-serving. We may put in fewer hours than we know we agreed to and figure out a way to justify that to ourselves. Consequently we will, no doubt, become a little defensive when a warden notices our frequent absences. We may mishandle the conversation with the head of the Altar Guild. Her displeasure and our defensiveness may result in people taking sides in a war that never needed to be fought. We may then find we need to tell ourselves that this showdown needed to happen. Probably there won't be anyone watching who can point out how we could have done it better, and so we won't learn what we could have learned from the situation.

To be sure that we will become leaders who practice mutual accountability, we need to instill in ourselves some good habits that will help keep us grounded. Keeping Lord Acton's dictum on power in mind, we need to find ways to hold ourselves accountable in the exercise of our power so that we are in less danger of being corrupted by it. And we need to remember that we *do* have power. It may seem appropriately modest to protest that you don't have any power, but it is actually pretty dangerous. Not recognizing the powers of our office and of our personality makes it easy to pretend that we don't have to be that careful about what we do or say with others, because after all, we have no power. It is yet one more way we can get ourselves into the kind of one-way relationships that we can justify to ourselves.

What follow in this chapter are some suggestions that might assist us. Some are suggestions for developing habits, such as saying the daily office, tithing, and apologizing frequently. Others are intentions to keep specifically in mind, like being authentic and working hard. There is no one single way of developing these; our personalities and our lives are not that uniform. But perhaps through my discussion of these topics you will see areas you want to address in your life. Just thinking about them has reminded me afresh of how wrong it would be to let you think I had all these good habits and intentions under control myself!

WORK HARD. DO YOUR JOB EVEN IF IT IS BENEATH YOU

A colleague told a group of newly ordained priests, "Clergy come in two varieties—workaholics and bone-lazy." There is just enough truth in that to make it worth repeating. Years ago, as we were moving furniture in the undercroft after a dinner so we could set up for choir practice, the rector of the parish in which I was confirmed said, "You can't be an Episcopalian if you aren't willing to move tables and chairs."

One of the tensions in ministry is that the number of tasks one could do is nearly infinite, but there is actually very little that one *must* do. This is bad news for both the workaholics and those inclined to be lazy, because there is usually nothing in the structure that will save us from our worst tendencies. There is nothing that will get the workaholics to slow down, and little that will kick the others into gear.

In addition the work of ministry covers so many areas that no one I know can do them all with equal proficiency or equal satisfaction. Pastor, teacher, preacher, liturgist, board president, administrator, organizer, building superintendent, supervisor, manager, visionary—everything has to be covered, but no one, workaholic or lazy, is going to like all of it or be good at all of it. It is tempting, therefore, to pay little attention to the parts we don't like and the parts we don't feel good at. Workaholics will busy themselves with other tasks so they never have time for those parts. Procrastinators will have no trouble avoiding what they don't like.

I once heard a priest who didn't want to work with youth say to the vestry that if they wanted to have a youth group, it was their job, not his. Perhaps this was not the most effective way to hold up the importance of youth work and inspire someone to volunteer. Nor is it quite true. We don't have to do everything, but it is part of our job to see, as much as possible, that everything gets done. In much the same way a museum director does not need to repair damage to the artifacts herself, but seeing that the collection is conserved is part of her job.

I say "as much as possible," because in many situations the community is not yet ready to move ahead on some aspect of parish life. Maybe you know you need to get a Sunday school started again, for example, but the kids and potential teachers just aren't there. Or maybe there has been absolutely no response to your adult education initiatives. Maybe you need to raise capital funds but there is no enthusiasm at all for a campaign. That's okay—if you keep your eyes focused on where you want to go, you'll recognize and explore any little opportunity that arises that can help nudge things in that direction. Without this focus on your goals, you shouldn't be surprised if the congregation does not go anywhere.

It is a common temptation, especially with the current emphasis on lay ministry, for clergy to define what they don't want to do as the job of the laity. For some it might be the upkeep of the buildings, for others keeping track of finances, and for others Christian education, youth work, or even pastoral care of the sick. Some clergy feel so awkward talking about money that they say that stewardship formation is the laity's job. So if there are parts of the job that we are currently defining as "lay ministries," it is worth asking ourselves if that is really so or if it is some task that we want to avoid. And if it is something that could or should be done by laypeople, do we adequately support the work they're doing, or treat it as something unimportant because we don't want to get involved? I am not advocating that we become control freaks who try to do everything; a lot of clergy tend to be a bit too controlling. So it may be a good idea to back off from time to time, but that isn't the same as defining what we don't want to do as the laity's job.

There may also be parts of the job we think are beneath us. If we have those feelings at all, they are worth examining because it is a red flag. Long before I was ordained, I worked for a couple of years as an appointee in a local elected official's office as the liaison for certain populations in the community. After about eighteen months, I was feeling pretty good about the work I was doing and the agencies and organizations I worked with seemed to find me a useful resource. Then at some reception in the office, I was assigned to work the coat check.

As I reflected on my negative reaction to this, I came to think that I felt this way because my motivation to do that job was the status I thought it gave me. It upset me to have that taken away. If we are not doing the job we really want to do, our motivation will likely be money or position or some other external gain. I've never had a similar reaction to anything that needed to be done in my work around the church; I may not have wanted to do something, but that is not the same as feeling that a particular job is beneath me.

Last Sunday I carried chairs down from the gym to the coffee hour room to help get things ready. Of course, I would probably begin to feel differently about it if I had to carry the chairs down every week. Many of us clergy are the ones who have to set things up, get the furnace going, clear the snow, and so on. I suggest that we need to be attentive to how such duties make us feel. If they make us feel taken advantage of, it is worth inquiring why. Does it make us feel that way because our heart isn't in what we're doing? Or is it related to the discussion in Chapter 3 about making sure that the circumstances of our employment meet the criteria of basic fairness? We can feel exploited because we are doing a job we don't really like or because we *are* exploited. Regardless of why, the net result is the same—a kind of toxin that seeps into everything, warping our vocation. So it is worthwhile to see if there's a way to address any unfairness in how things are set up, as well as to pay close attention to those feelings. If there is any way at all to get to the point where you can do (most of) what you need to do with a willing heart, it is worth trying to get there.

RECITE THE DAILY OFFICE, SAY YOUR PRAYERS AND STUDY THE BIBLE

It is important to be regular in prayer and study. That is part of our ordination vows and, if we've been instituted in a parish, part of the prayer we said at that service. It is also important that it not become something about which we constantly fret and make ourselves feel guilty. Some of us like routines and are easily able to make the daily office part of them; others of us don't do routines that well. I have a set routine every morning, but if I'm away from home, I find it very difficult to say the office because that morning pattern is thrown off.

How we pray, when we pray, how much we pray, what other study we do, what books we read—all these will differ from person to person. Differences in personality type make certain kinds of prayer easier for some and unrewarding for others. There is not one way to do this, but it is necessary to do it, partly because we promised to and partly because we need to. If we don't maintain a vital connection with the living Word, our ability to minister will wither. Perhaps more than one of us can attest to that from the dry periods we may have experienced.

The results of our life of prayer and study cannot be measured, but it will be apparent to those we serve whether we are maintaining our end of a vital spiritual connection with God. I don't mean ostentatious acts of piety or cultivating a "church" voice. I'm talking about the wisdom, patience, and insight that can come only through that connection.

Though the results can't be measured, the time we spend in prayer and study and what we do during that time can, so it is an area that can produce guilt if it does not measure up to what we think it should or what we imagine that others achieve. Some of us are a little compulsive, but on the other hand, some of us may not have developed any regular prayer and study time at all. If we are not happy with how this is going, perhaps a trusted colleague or a spiritual director can help us move to a different place. But here is the point: a non-existent or perfunctory spiritual life is a warning sign we need to pay attention to.

GET YOUR MONEY IN ORDER

This is part of the craft of leadership that may seem unrelated to the main task, especially since many of us are not gifted financial managers. However, if your financial life is not in order, the disorder is almost sure to spread to other parts of your life. It is difficult to concentrate on the challenges of our ministry if we are anxious about collection agencies and our credit rating. Severe financial pressure can also lead us to misuse church funds, especially if there are not adequate internal controls in how the parish handles its money. For example, we may start to pay for personal items out of our discretionary fund if it is a separate account on which we are the only signatory and which is never audited. And if we are not formed as generous stewards, when we speak about others' giving, it just won't ring true, and it won't move our hearers' hearts.

Here, as in so many other areas, we will not be able to do everything at once. The point is to turn ourselves so that we face in the direction we want to go. If we truly intend to pay off our consumer debt, we will do so faster than if we haven't adopted that as a goal we truly want to accomplish. Christian formation is about the healing of the will. We will do the right things more reliably if those are the things that we really want and intend to do.

Tithing

I consider tithing to be the most important part of my rule of life. I began it about thirty years ago when my partner and I were in a very serious financial bind, and I felt I had done all I could do to address it. Ten percent worked out to be more than double the amount of our weekly pledge, and we were behind with that. Two things happened as soon as I wrote that first check. First, I was conscious of trusting God in a way I never had before because of the larger amount I gave. Second, I realized that because I had given off the top, before we paid any other bills, the amount I had given didn't feel at all burdensome. It actually felt like less than the weekly pledge I couldn't pay.

The main thing was to change the order in which we spent our money. If you give every week whether you've received any money that week or not, and if what you give is a set dollar amount not connected to the money you received, it will feel as though you're paying a bill that comes due every week. Giving a proportion off the top changes everything, however, because it changes the experience. Giving a percentage off the top only when you actually receive money feels like you're making a thank offering in direct proportion to what you just received.

In the decades we have been tithing we have "abased and abounded" to a great extent, and through it all there has always been enough without a whole lot left over. Giving the tithe first thing every time we get money is a reaffirmation of an act of faith that puts God in charge of making it all work out. And I have never been as anxious about money as I was before I made this change.

I also know it was easier for me to begin to tithe because I had been brought up having to put ten percent of my Saturday allowance into the envelope for church the next day. I had stopped doing it when I left home, but the pattern had been imprinted. Perhaps without that childhood experience, I wouldn't have thought of tithing as a way out of our financial crisis. However you do it, I suggest from my own personal experience that you try to make whatever you give the church a percentage off the top of what you have just received. If it feels burdensome, reduce the percentage until your pattern of giving feels liberating. Over time you may find that it is not that difficult to give ten percent because it is what you really want to do. That was how my mother got back to tithing in the years after the upset of my father's early death.

I have come to believe that practicing proportional giving is at least as important as our life of prayer. Giving generously was not part of our ordination vows, but you can tell whether someone gives generously in the same way you can tell whether he or she has a vital prayer life. The results are apparent in how we conduct our ministry. This practice will have a direct impact on how you talk about stewardship formation and the annual pledge drive. If you've found a way to give that has unleashed your desire to be generous while reducing your anxiety about money, you won't feel a bit shy about sharing that good news with others. Finally, please, never suggest that anyone else do something that you are not doing.

Taxes

Clergy taxes are different from just about anyone else's. One reason is that when we are working as clergy we are considered W-2 employees for income tax purposes, but we are considered self-employed for Social Security tax purposes, so our employers cannot withhold that tax, match it, and send it in along with the withheld federal income tax. We must make arrangements to see that those estimated taxes are paid, either by making the quarterly payments or by asking the church to withhold additional federal income tax to cover the self-employment tax obligation.

Church-provided housing and the tax-excludable parsonage allowance under Section 107 of the tax law are additional complications. We owe self-employment tax on everything, including the fair value of church-provided housing and utilities, but we do not owe income tax on the housing. Honoraria you take as income, furthermore, need to be reported on Schedule C, another thing you didn't have to deal with before ordination.

I have seen the self-employment tax be an ugly surprise for the newly ordained. The IRS will cut you a break the first year you owe self-employment tax, but after that you need to make sure you are getting them enough money to cover both the self-employment tax and the income tax obligations. The self-employment tax is a big bite, and for most of us it is much more than we owe in income tax.

Someone may have told you that clergy can exempt them-selves from the self-employment tax by exempting themselves from the entire Social Security and Medicare system. It is true that an ordained person can file IRS Form 4361 within two years of beginning to earn self-employment income as an ordained person. You can apply for the exemption by claiming that, on the basis of a conscientious objection or religious principles, you are opposed "to any public insurance that makes payments in the event of death, disability, old age, or retirement; or that makes payments toward the cost of, or provides services for, medical care." You must also certify that you have informed the body that ordained you of your objection to government funded pensions, insurance, and health care.

You may be opposed to paying the 15.3 percent self-employment tax, but that is not the same thing as a conscientious objection to government insurance or medical care. One priest told me his ordaining bishop encouraged him to request the exemption because the priest already had enough credited service in the Social Security system from secular employment to entitle him to a pension and Medicare coverage, but I cannot agree that beginning one's ministry with a lie to the federal government is a good idea.

I would also urge you not to play games with the tax-excludable housing allowance. You cannot exclude from income tax more than your eligible housing-related expenses, and in no case can the excludable amount exceed the fair rental value of the house you are providing for yourself, or, in the case of church supplied housing, the value your furnishings added to the fair rental value of the house.

See if your diocesan office offers a clergy tax workshop. Find a tax preparer who understands clergy taxes. Call the Pension Fund's consultants who can answer questions. Get to the point where whoever does the money in your household has a fairly firm grasp of these matters. There are at least two very good reasons not to cut corners here. First, you will sleep better knowing that you can withstand an IRS audit. Not surprisingly, tax returns that include Schedule SE and Schedule C are audited more frequently than simple returns that report only W-2 income.

Second, what we do and what we fail to do both form our character. If we knowingly cheat on our taxes, or if we end up cheating out of willful ignorance, it will have an effect on us and on our ministry. It becomes a bad secret that will surely warp us

Debts

Since consumer debt is a lucrative business for financial institutions, they work hard to keep us in debt at high interest rates. We tend to incur significant consumer debt—student loans, car loans, and credit card purchases—as we are getting our adult lives set up, because most of us don't have much saved. For example, when the renovation of our kitchen got out of control in the mid-1980s because of a contractor who took the money and ran, we had to finance a great deal of the work on a credit card, and it took many years to get rid of that balance.

So we incur debt for useful things. As money gets tighter, however, we also tend to incur debt for things we don't need. The act of charging something, like drink or drugs or sex, displaces temporarily feelings of anxiety and sadness even though the effect of our actions is additional future anxiety. So a "mid-range" goal of our personal financial plan must be to pay off credit card debt, the most expensive way of borrowing money. There are better things we can do with that money, such as save for retirement. I've had the opportunity to help some clergy consolidate their debt and get control of it. Afterward they felt much relieved, and you will, too.

Saving for Retirement

Many mainline clergy are fortunate because the denominational pension funds may still offer the defined-benefit pension plans that have virtually disappeared from the private sector. Clergy can expect a substantial percentage of the income they will need in retirement to come from their pension plan and from Social Security.

However, those sources will probably not be enough. First, defined benefit plans work best when you have a lot of years in the system. Forty years at $40,000 will produce a bigger pension than fifteen years at $100,000. Since today many clergy are ordained in middle age, they won't have that many years of credited service, and the pension will replace a smaller percentage of their income. Second, in your "active retirement" years you will want additional money for travel and other activities you'll have the leisure to enjoy. Planners tell us that we'll want to have more income in retirement than we have while working. The way to make up the shortfall is to save for retirement.

Clergy are fortunate in this as well because the contributions we make to a 403(b) plan are completely untaxed. Regular employees and their employers must pay the Social Security and Medicare tax on their 403(b) contributions, but because clergy are self-employed for Social Security tax purposes, our contributions are wholly pre-tax. This means that for many of us it costs fifty cents or less in take-home pay to save one dollar for retirement, because our final earnings can be taxed at 50 percent, when you add up the SE tax, and all income taxes on the last dollars you earn.

Make sure your pension assessments are paid so you get the years of credited service that you have earned. I know plenty of dedicated priests who, filled with youthful zeal, allowed the pension assessments to go unpaid in the early years of their ministry. Your perspective will change, I assure you, and, as you come to realize the effect this will have on your retirement, you will come to resent that you were taken advantage of. Spare yourself that bitterness and the dangerous ways you might develop to compensate for the injustice.

There are plenty of resources to assist you with this. In the Episcopal Church the Pension Fund runs periodic overnight "Planning for Tomorrow" conferences. Financial planning is a major feature of the week-long CREDO program. Pension Fund staff are available for individual consultation and there are online tools on the Pension Fund's website (www.cpg.org) that will help.

GET YOUR SEX LIFE IN ORDER AND KEEP
YOUR PROMISES

For many of us this is easy. We have a physically and emotionally fulfilling relationship with someone we love. We get a kick out of being together, and we are both eager to listen to what the other wants. We may notice attractive people in passing, but we never have any kind of desire to break our promises.

For others it is more complicated, at least at certain times. If we are not in a relationship before ordination, it can be difficult to form one afterward. Gone are the days when mothers could fix their daughters up with the new curate. To date someone in your parish is now viewed as so dangerous that it requires the bishop's consent according to most sexual misconduct policies. And if you are in a relationship, things can get bumpy as well. Channels of communication can dry up, or maybe disappointments with your sex life can't be worked out, so you stop talking about it, and soon there is no sex life. Or your spouse stops asking you about your day because you've frequently indicated you're too exhausted and irritable to talk about it, so when you want to talk, there's nobody to listen. Or the two of you can't come to an agreement about how to handle your money, and the arguments that begin over money spin out of control. "Let's stop," the wife says to her husband in a *New Yorker* cartoon, "before we say a lot of things we mean."

In that kind of relationship, it can occur to us that we are not getting the satisfaction we used to get or think we should be getting. But there can be other things as well, including mid-life fears, career disappointments, financial problems, or simply an irresistable impulse to give into temptation. A friend once told me that early in his marriage he was suddenly presented with the possibility of an immediate sexual encounter and stammered out, "I can't. I have a wife who loves me." But he also told me that years later, under different circumstances, he had not only accepted, but had sought out, similar encounters.

The word we commonly use now to describe the appropriate limits of our conduct is "boundaries," and it is apt. Whether we are talking about money, sex, or alcohol, moving past those boundaries can be a vertiginous experience. Another friend said he thought he was going only half a step beyond the fence, but when he finally turned around, he discovered that all places outside the boundary are equally far removed from home.

There may be ways to repair and rebuild your relationship; there may not be. In some circumstances separation is indicated; in others that may not be desired. Deep satisfaction with your relationship might not be possible, but we need to figure out a way to live inside the boundaries.

Don't Drink to Excess and Get Help if You Do

Some of us enjoy an occasional drink and some of us enjoy a good bit more than that. Drinking is another area of life that has boundaries around it, but the boundaries are often harder to discern than those around sex and money. Alcoholism may be broadly defined as the persistent use of alcohol despite negative consequences. What constitutes the overuse of alcohol, along with the frequency and regularity of its use needed to develop alcoholism, vary among individuals, so that what is dangerous for one person may not be so for another. It is easy to deceive ourselves when we try to define "negative consequences." There are easily accessible online questionnaires that can administer a reality check. We don't need to have lost our job or alienated our family in order to have an alcohol problem; in fact many active alcoholics are gainfully employed.

Over time, however, there will probably be mounting evidence that our drinking is affecting the rest of our lives. It is usually difficult for us to come to that realization, however, despite any number of indications. Drinking is something we often do with others. Among men, straight or gay, the culture of drinking is often tied to perceptions of manliness: "real men" can drink with no ill effects. If it is hard to admit to ourselves that we have a problem, it is even harder for many of us to say that to our drinking buddies. Of course, drinking alone has its own difficulties.

I'm not sure if it is possible for us to drink too much over time without its affecting the job we do, any more than it is possible for a lawyer or doctor to drink too much with no effect on the practice of his or her profession. If we want to get out in one piece, it is a good idea to pay attention to this if we think we may have a problem.

BE A TEAM PLAYER AND GO TO CONVENTION, CLERGY CONFERENCES, CLERICUS/DEANERY MEETINGS, ORDINATIONS, INSTITUTIONS, AND RETIREMENTS

Since the church is the gathered assembly, it does not work if the church's leaders avoid gatherings. No matter the polity of your denomination, the ministry is a collegial undertaking. We benefit from attending gatherings outside our congregation because such events simultaneously remind us of the collegial nature of our work and allow us a physical expression of that collegiality.

I will freely grant that many, if not most, of these gatherings can be downright tedious. Special services are often disjointed and usually go on too long. Clergy meetings are not always scintillating, and there aren't enough air-conditioned churches in the Northeast. Theologian and preacher Will Willimon in a commencement address at a Presbyterian seminary said that the principal reason to require Greek and Hebrew is to get ordinands used to spending a lot of time doing things that serve no apparent purpose. Of course there is a purpose to these meetings and services that is apparent and important: we are a team, so we must play together. We get a chance to see colleagues we don't often see. We can usually learn something if we keep our ears open. No matter how long or hot it was, we will almost always find ourselves saying, "Well, it was nice to talk to Bill." And we often feel as though something in us has been refreshed.

A pattern of avoiding gatherings outside the parish is a danger signal. If you find that you're always unavailable to attend meetings and special services, it might be a good idea to think about why that is. If you really are that busy, maybe that's too busy. Does that much in your parish really depend on you being there all the time? Really? Is that a good idea? If you go to a colleague's institution, you'll just be with the other clergy; you won't be presiding. Is that the problem? We will not be able to get to everything, but it is a good practice to get to the ones we can.

BE ACCOUNTABLE AND HONEST IN ALL RELATIONSHIPS

One of the major ideas in this book is that mutual accountability in all our relationships is necessary for effective leadership. We simply cannot be good leaders if we are unapproachable or defensive, or if we don't have people's backs. If that is true of us, we will not hear the truth and morale will be very low. Especially if we make communication difficult, we might be able to convince ourselves that we are justified in what we're doing and the way we're doing it, but we won't fool anyone else. We will damage and weaken the institution we are supposed to be strengthening.

After all, we have almost limitless possibilities to get it right. Every encounter is a chance to be open. Every conversation is an opportunity to show that we are not overly impressed with ourselves and that we are responsibly aware of the power we have. Every meeting is a chance to encourage a candid discussion of what will be in the institution's long-term best interests, even if it means we don't get our way. Maybe the ideas of others are better than ours.

We have the same number of possibilities to strike a sour note or get it completely wrong. I am not suggesting an obsessive examination of our conduct. We know while a conversation is going on how well we're handling it. If we realize afterwards that we messed it up, we'll want to acknowledge that at some point so the right kind of relationship can be re-established. It may be serious enough to call the person right away, or perhaps an e-mail is sufficient. It may be minor enough that the next time we see the person, we can say, "When I said X, I didn't mean to imply Y. I'm sorry if that's how it came across." Lots of times the person will not have taken it wrong, but on those occasions when we have rankled someone, a "pre-emptive apology" is more precious than pearls.

There are also little things we can do to collect ourselves before an important conversation. Long before I was ordained, when my partner was being called as the rector of a parish, we knew they were offering less than the minimum compensation. I called the diocesan office for the first time and asked the staff person then in charge of these things for a copy of the guidelines. "I will not send them to you," the person said. Confused, I asked, "But aren't they adopted by convention? Aren't they public?" "We don't get involved in that," came the answer and then the click of the phone being hung up. There was, as you might imagine, an unpleasant back story that we didn't learn for some time.

In the years I worked at the diocesan office, I remembered that conversation almost every time I picked up the phone. Every call gave me the opportunity to get it right. Whatever the matter at hand, I wanted the caller at the end to feel better about being part of the Diocese of New York than before our conversation. Though I frequently did not achieve this goal, I think it helped to have that conscious intention. The former assistant bishop in our diocese, E. Don Taylor, told me once that he made the sign of the cross before picking up the phone because he never knew what he might be dealing with. Perhaps the priest who sponsored you for ordination had a way with people that you want to emulate, so getting into the habit of thinking, "Let me handle this the way Jane would" might help you imitate her. Or perhaps you had a negative experience like mine. Resolving at the beginning of every conversation not to treat another as you were treated might help keep that from happening.

APOLOGIZE FREQUENTLY AND SINCERELY

It costs nothing to say you're sorry. On a scale of 0 to 6, with "humble and strong" at one end and "arrogant and weak" at the other, try to figure out where you stand. How easy is it for you to apologize simply and sincerely for a mistake? Let's say you have made a calendar error that causes you to miss something you had promised to attend. How easy is it for you to take responsibility for the error without having to blame someone else? If you can simply apologize with sincerity and try to figure out a way to make it up to those you have disappointed, that's a 0 or a 1. If you hear yourself saying something about the pressure of work, that's not so good; you're at 2 or 3. If you hear yourself blaming your Blackberry, sorry, you're at least at 4. If you feel the need to blame your assistant, you've jumped to 6. If your response is to pretend that you had called and told the organizers you wouldn't be able to come, you are very far gone indeed.

A priest I know had a bishop coming who had promised to be at all the services. She didn't start the eight o'clock service for over half an hour, waiting for the bishop to arrive. When the bishop did come, he said he had told the priest a few days before that he would not be coming for the early service, and my friend was forced to apologize to the congregation for "her" mistake. Of course that conversation never happened; that particular ploy was part of that bishop's modus operandi. My friend had experienced it on other occasions, as had others.

Now let's say the parish administrator actually made the mistake. Can you apologize to the people you have disappointed and take responsibility for the mistake, or do you tell them that your assistant was to blame? If you find it necessary to blame your staff in front of others, even when it was the staff person's mistake, you are at 6. Leaders who do not have the backs of the people who work for them are arrogant and weak, in addition to being terrible bosses. Morale won't be high in your shop.

And even if you have your staff's back in public, how do you treat them when outsiders aren't present? How are you going to speak to your assistant about that mistake? One friend who works for the bishop of another diocese said that her boss was supportive of the staff in public, but that in the office it was a completely different story, with lots of yelling and temper tantrums. How you treat the people who work for you is important enough that part of the last chapter of this book will be devoted to it. There really is a craft to staff supervision. It is not something you can just suddenly do because you've been elected a rector or a bishop.

It is important to be able to apologize sincerely and without defensiveness for real mistakes, including the mistakes of others if they work for you. It is also important, I think, to be able to apologize sincerely for things that are not your fault. If someone gets upset about a blooper in the newsletter prepared by volunteers, a wine cruet not put out on the credence table, or a miscommunication or misunderstanding that does not involve you—at the very least it doesn't cost anything to express your sincere regret that the person is upset. And if it does feel that such an apology would cost us something, perhaps we'd be humbler and stronger without that something anyway.

I do not mean that you should take on others' responsibilities, make yourself feel guilty, enable bad behavior, or apologize insincerely. Apologizing is a good way to practice not being defensive. And it is extremely disarming. I've seen apologizing without guilt or blame calm many troubled waters. Actually, strategic apologizing, like strategic generosity, is an effective way to model good behavior.

Most mistakes and miscommunications are systemic problems anyway, not one person's fault. People will make mistakes. It is our job as leaders to figure out if there are procedures we can put into place that will catch mistakes before they are a problem. In my twenties I worked in an office with about fifteen very excitable people. When something went wrong, there would be shouting matches about who was to blame. They never agreed, of course, but when people felt they had made their point loudly enough, everybody just walked away, and the problem was still there. Those years taught me that guilt and blame are useless occupations. The point surely is to analyze the problem and try to find a way not only to fix it now, but to prevent it from recurring. And if you are overseeing the system, then you can certainly apologize sincerely for not having thought to make the system better before the snafu.

It can be difficult to get ourselves and others to think of how a system can be fixed rather than of whom we could be blaming for the problem. Finding something you can honestly apologize for without guilt or blame is a good way to get started.

BE AUTHENTIC IN YOUR LIFE AND IN YOUR
PREACHING

I don't know how it is in your part of the world, but some of my colleagues and I keep finding out that people who don't belong to a church don't expect much of the clergy. It is not unusual for people to say to a priest, "You're really nice," as if a nice priest were a surprising thing to find in a church. We have heard enough stories to know that it is priests who have caused people to think that way, and we ourselves are probably responsible for making others feel that the church is a great disappointment. It is not a bad thing to try to be that surprisingly nice priest when someone comes by or phones the church.

What turns us off about other people, whether ordained or not? One older lady who liked to tell her stories met another older lady who was equally devoted to telling her own stories. "Well, she had a lot to say for herself," the first lady sniffed as we were leaving. That leads me to think that the main thing we don't like to see in another person is our own besetting weakness. On the other hand, another older lady I know almost always makes a deep impression on others, not because she is so vivacious, but simply because she is sincerely interested in the other person, so a ten-minute conversation with her makes people feel that they've really been listened to.

Even in a fairly brief exchange, if we listen carefully and respond thoughtfully to what the person is saying—and not saying—we can often get past the rote stories people tell about themselves and hear something of the real story. The fourth chapter of John's gospel purports to contain the entire exchange between Jesus and the Samaritan woman at the well. Immediately after Jesus tells her that he is the Christ, the text says, "Just then his disciples came." On the basis of the conversation recorded the woman tells her fellow townspeople, "Come, see a man who told me all that I ever did." Jesus had not actually told her anything about her life except her marital history. The right kind of conversation does not have to be lengthy in order to forge a real connection.

Probably the most important thing is for us to keep our story from getting in the way of someone else's. What stories have we heard a colleague tell or told ourselves tell that gets in the way of another's story? When we are wearing clericals at the church we may feel a need to communicate to others that we are in charge, or that we know what we are doing, or that we're not ashamed of a building that is shabbier than it should be, or that the congregation is doing better than it really is, or that we're more important than we seem to be, or that our life is more together than it might actually be, or that we are smarter or better informed, or that we are really too busy for this conversation. There are many verbal and non-verbal means of bringing inauthenticity into the interchange, and the more we do that, the less effectively we will represent Christ and his church to that person.

The farther we let ourselves get from the reality of our lives, the less effective we will be. One priest, for example, who lived apart from his wife for several years, made frequent reference in his sermons to the joys of wedded bliss. If he'd handled it differently, people might have been sympathetic to someone going through a difficulty many of them had experienced, but his refusal to be authentic in public or in private and what seemed like blatant insincerity were intolerable to many and contributed to an ugly dénouement to his ministry in that congregation. We can make terrible mistakes and still minister effectively, but only if we can acknowledge the situation with the right combination of humility, sincerity, and self-respect.

One difficulty for those in the ordained ministry is that our lives are samples of the product we're selling. Christianity is about how God transforms lives and about the role our repentance and conversion plays in that transformation. None of us will be perfect examples, but we will serve as examples whether we want to or not. If we don't keep it real, we will not be efective; people will see only how what we say is disconnected from what we do. If we can keep it real, most people will forgive our shortcomings because they can glimpse what our lives are trying to point to.

This may also be a way we can help bridge the gap that has opened in the last generation or so between spirituality and religion. Why does one quarter of the population describe itself as "spiritual but not religious"? It may be that from their experiences of religion, or from what they've gleaned about it from the culture, many people do not expect the Christian church to be a place to go if you're looking for an authentic spiritual experience. The perceptions of Christianity on the part of those who have never attended church are no doubt informed to a great degree by the negative experiences of their peers, by jokes, and by the media's reporting of the religious right. The mainline churches have a very different story to tell, but we need authenticity to tell it effectively. When the gospels say that Jesus taught "with authority," they mean something quite different from the authority that comes with having an office. In fact, Jesus' authority is contrasted with that of the scribes, who were the ones authorized to teach. The authority ascribed to Jesus has much more to do with the sheer transparency of his words. No cant, no posturing, no extraneous matter, no distractions of personality—nothing got in the way of Jesus' direct communication with his hearers.

I want to suggest that as leaders in the church we can help others who are looking for the experience of acceptance and connection to find it in our congregations. To do this, I think we need to stay rooted and grounded in the experiential aspects of our own faith, and we need to find ways of relating those aspects with authenticity to the experiences of those who are seeking.

DON'T DISMISS THE TRADITION. WRESTLE WITH IT UNTIL IT BLESSES YOU

The great historian Jaroslav Pelikan said, "Tradition is the living faith of the dead; traditionalism is the dead faith of the living." When as a young adult I was teaching Sunday school, if all I could think to say in answer to a question was "The church teaches..." I felt I had failed. It meant that the teaching wasn't yet my living faith; it still belonged to others.

My observation and experience tell me that we do best when we stick to the "tradition" with a capital T, or what has been called the "core doctrine" of the church, and struggle with it until we understand how generations of Christians have been able to find it their living faith. The articles of faith that "modern" people have problems with—the virgin birth, the resurrection, and the ascension—have been problematic from the beginning. First-century people knew as well as we do where babies come from, and they also knew that dead is dead. These were not discoveries of the Enlightenment or of higher biblical criticism. It isn't necessary to be able to explain how these things work in modern categories any more than it was necessary to explain how they worked in the light of ancient categories. It is necessary, I think, to be able to insist on the astounding claim that God became human and that that human being's body died and was raised to a new life into which we are incorporated through baptism and nurtured in the eucharist.

The idea that pre-modern people were so credulous that they could easily believe in Jesus' incarnation and resurrection is simply false, a straw man created in the nineteenth century so that modern scholarship could knock it down. After the resurrection skeptics told the story that Mary was impregnated by a Roman soldier and that Jesus' disciples stole his body from the tomb. We do not need modern "scientific" revisionists to speculate that the resurrection appearances were events in the disciples' minds. That is the easy way out. It is more interesting and much more compelling to think through Jesus' miracles and find the connection between people's experiences today than it is to try to explain that everybody brought food with them to the feeding of the five thousand. (The Bible actually indicates that they did not.) It is better and potentially far more life-changing to work through the implications of a real bodily resurrection than to say that we are dealing with the disciples' vivid memories.

There is much to be gained from struggling with the parts of Christian tradition that we don't take to right away, but little use in simply rejecting something that does not comport with our assumptions. When we have worked it through sufficiently, most likely we'll end up able to distinguish the treasure we want to keep from the "earthen vessel" that contains it, and we might be transformed in the process.

"But these are metaphors!" you might exclaim. Certainly. All language is metaphorical, but when I was translating Virgil in high school, my teacher said to use the shortest, most concrete nouns and verbs in my translations, not abstractions. And remember, metaphors are not similes. A simile likens something to something else, as in "Your lips are like cream." A metaphor says that something *is* something else, as in "This is my body. This is my blood." Stick with the concrete meaning and work it through. Making the tradition our own means to take seriously C. S. Lewis's suggestion that theological English needs to be translated into the vernacular. If you can't say what you mean without theological language, you have not thought it through:

> Any fool can write learned language. The vernacular is the real test. If you can't turn your faith into it, then either you don't understand it or you don't believe it.[1]

In the Acts of the Apostles, the believers speak of what they have "seen and heard." If our faith can't be expressed in terms accessible to our hearers, the tradition is only repeated, not effectively appropriated.

Doing that work also holds you accountable to both the Bible and Christian tradition. Without that accountability it is as bad as any one-way relationship. We are not smarter than the tradition; we are not "above" the rubrics in the prayer book. Not only is it a bad example of Christian leadership to give the impression that you know more than all who have gone before, it is also not true. This is not a call to any kind of fundamentalism or doctrinal rigidity. It is, I think, a call to the same kind of mutual accountability that I have called for throughout this book. The tradition cannot bless you if you walk away from it. Grab hold of it and wrestle a blessing from it.

REMEMBER THAT IT IS NOT ALL ABOUT YOU

I once knew a priest who was deeply narcissistic and truly seemed to believe that it was all about him. That belief communicated itself unmistakably in everything he did. For example, it was impossible to attend any service he conducted without being constantly made aware of his presence—people called it "the Jimmy show." He seldom attended a service at which he wasn't officiating, and when he did, always entered late or left early in ways that called attention to himself. Similarly, a bishop who was scheduled to meet with a group of clergy and lay leaders deputed a staff member to inform the group in advance that they should not ask the bishop any questions that might upset him or make him angry. If the president of the United States can't avoid difficult questions at press conferences, what in the world can give a bishop such a breathtaking sense of entitlement? How can such a priest with such a sense of entitlement believe himself to be acting in accordance with his ordination vows and the teachings of Jesus?

The church is structured in a way that makes self-importance and feelings of entitlement an easy trap to fall into. Clergy in charge of congregations are often in the spotlight, so it is easy to begin to think that the show is about you and that you deserve the best dressing room. Even if you start off with modesty and work hard, people will begin to look to you, admire you, compliment you, and defer to you, so eventually it is easy to think you deserve that kind of reverence no matter how you act.

Ending up self-involved and feeling entitled is, you might say, the default mode of power. I know some people for whom humble and strong leadership seems to be natural, but for most of us it takes constant, daily work to hold ourselves accountable in such a way that humble and strong leadership becomes second nature. The work is made easier by establishing habits and habitual intentions such as those outlined here. If it seems too laborious to make this effort, please remember that the costs of leadership that is not humble and strong end up being higher than we expect. We will pay some of those costs as our vocations are twisted beyond recognition. The institutions we lead will pay even more dearly as staffers are demoralized, members become disaffected, opportunities are missed, and a legacy created that our successors will not thank us for having to deal with after we are gone.

End Notes:

1. C. S. Lewis, in a letter to the editor in *The Christian Century*, 31 December 1958, 1006–7.

CHAPTER FIVE

LEADERSHIP IN ACTION

Moses' father-in-law said to him, "What you are doing is not good. You will surely wear yourself out, both you and these people with you. For the task is too heavy for you; you cannot do it alone." (Ex. 18:17–18)

MOST CLERGY IN charge of congregations have two roles with regard to the institutional life of the parish, chairing the governing board of the congregation and functioning as the executive director. Too many people like to say that the church must operate differently from secular organizations. I think this confuses the purpose of the church with its organizational functioning, so I have deliberately used non-church terms. The purpose of the church is the conversion and transformation of people through their relationship with the risen body of Christ. As an institution, however, the church functions like other organizations; it has structures, roles, and procedures that order its life. It owns property, holds endowments, maintains buildings, and raises and spends money.

It is not a denial but rather an affirmation of the spiritual purpose of the church to pay proper attention to these matters. As I pointed out in Chapter 1, the treasure would be lost without the earthen vessels. There are lots of reasons people say they don't want the church to operate as secular organizations do. Sometimes it is a longing to be part of a transformative and transformed organization, but at other times it is something less laudable. To say "God will provide" is easier than doing the hard work of being a good steward of what is in your care. Sometimes the motive is control, such as the warden who said the parish shouldn't operate like other organizations because he wanted the vestry to exercise unlimited control over every aspect of the life of the congregation, including those areas canonically reserved to the priest.

If, however, you think the church should not be run like a business, you are correct. It should be run like a not-for-profit organization because that is what it is. On an organizational level the church is governed by structures that are almost identical to those of all other not-for-profit corporations such as universities, hospitals, cultural institutions, and service and community organizations. Like the church, these are all entities with a mission. Unlike many churches, most not-for-profits know that they need a well-run institution to facilitate the mission. The better we take care of the institution, and the more we act like Christians while we're doing it, the stronger our witness to the world will be.

As a human system, the church is very similar to any membership organization that holds frequent meetings of the members, like the Rotary Club or a garden club. That is why, absent effective leadership, congregations tend to function like clubs. Since the vestry and the clergy have different responsibilities, the system works well when each attends to its responsibilities and does not attempt to do the other's job. Although the duties are different, the areas of concern are the same. What both vestries and clergy deal with falls under these headings: leadership, development, fiduciary responsibilities, finances, personnel, and programs. The vestry and the clergy have different priorities, but since the first priority of both the vestry and the clergy is leadership, we will take that first. Then we will look at the appropriate ways vestries work in the remaining areas followed by the priorities clergy have in these areas.

LEADERSHIP

Effective leadership is the first priority of both the board and the clergy. Such leaders:

- keep their eyes on the long-term health of the institution;
- articulate a shared vision of where it can go;
- make things happen; and
- prepare to leave an institution stronger than it was when they began.

Leadership does *not* have to do with things like making as much money as you can, using the institution as a stepping stone in your career path, pretending things are better than they are, avoiding hard realities, or being someone other people have to manage around. That is why effective leadership has a fundamentally selfless quality, but if that selflessness is lacking, the results simply cannot be good. There was a bishop who at the beginning of his episcopate was unable to articulate anything that he wanted to accomplish, and he was very clear that he wanted to be paid a great deal more than his predecessor had received. That set the tone, and his episcopate unfolded as you might expect from that kind of beginning. That is a story that has been repeated in one way or another countless times at all levels of all organizations. It is one example of how being put in a leadership position does not necessarily make one a leader.

A generation ago congregations began to be encouraged to devise mission statements, and many people still seem to think that leadership cannot happen absent a mission statement or a strategic plan. In the last several years strategic planning has been the rage. In my opinion, based on my observation and experience, mission statements and strategic plans are of questionable value. In hundreds of meetings with many leadership groups on many different topics I have rarely seen the mission statement invoked, and I have never seen a mission statement or strategic plan be useful in the actual deliberations of the group. They are supposed to help us stick to the priorities we have defined, but mission statements are usually broad enough to encompass almost anything, and strategic plans are often so specific as to become quickly irrelevant or so vague as not to be plans.

I have seen vestries spend a great deal of time and energy working on the wording of a mission statement, with members making sure that their particular passion is in there. This makes them too long and diffuse. Shorter ones often quote or reference a phrase in a collect or the baptismal covenant, which is a nice idea but hardly complete. Any mission statement is either going to be partial, or it will be too broad to be of use.

The problem is that, in order to thrive, every parish must eventually do everything. Worship, formation, education, service to others—a Christian community needs to be involved in all of it. Other not-for-profits need a tight mission statement to keep their programs focused, but congregations cannot select parts of the Christian life to ignore. Therefore, a mission statement that excludes any of these areas is incomplete, but a planning session that results in a mission statement that says, "We'll do it all" may not have been a good use of people's time.

Not all group processes are useful. And no group process can be a substitute for leadership.

IDENTITY PRECEDES AND PRODUCES MISSION

In the same way that good leadership flows from someone who has become the right kind of person to exercise good leadership, mission comes from people who know themselves to be the kind of people who do mission. We don't worship, read the Bible, feed the hungry, or perform other acts of charity and justice because we are trying to avoid hell or win heaven, or because someone tells us we ought to. We do it because we have come to want to show the same reverence, generosity, and thoughtfulness in our lives that Jesus showed in his. We do it because of our identity as members of Jesus' risen body the church.

Every congregation already has a mission statement. The mission of the church is summed up in the catechism: "to restore all people to unity with God and each other in Christ." The church does this "as it prays and worships, proclaims the Gospel, and promotes justice, peace, and love" (BCP 855). Ideas about how the mission of the church can be furthered in a particular place and time will arise if there is an authentic desire to pursue that mission. It is probably not a good idea to be too specific in advance about how we want to pursue that mission; it is better to remain open to the opportunities God sends our way. In other words, keep talking about the kind of place you want the parish to be, and then be alive to opportunities that arise that will move you in that direction.

Focus on identity, and the ideas for how to express that identity will come. Effective leadership is fundamentally opportunistic; it recognizes opportunities as they arise and moves to take advantage of them. An inability or unwillingness to adjust to circumstances is not strength; it is a failure of strategic vision and leadership.

General Dwight D. Eisenhower said, "I have always found that plans are useless, but planning is indispensable." He was referring to how he prepared for battle, but it sums up concisely how leaders need to approach their task. The point is to think strategically, not necessarily to develop a step-by-step plan that events may make obsolete.

"Strategy" comes from the Greek word for "general," so strategy is originally a military idea. A general wants to win the battle and must decide, given the terrain, the weather, the strength of his opponents, and other variables, how to dispose his troops so he can accomplish that. An effective strategy is, therefore, specific to a certain situation and successful strategy has something to do with winning. Business strategies are about securing and maintaining a competitive advantage, and David La Piana incorporates that idea into his definition of not-for-profit strategy: "A coordinated set of actions aimed at creating and sustaining a competitive advantage in carrying out the nonprofit mission."[1] I don't recommend seeking competitive advantage; instead we should be pursuing excellence—expressing the mission of the church in the best, most effective way we can in our circumstances. So a strategy might be defined as "a set of actions aimed at enabling a congregation to achieve effectiveness and excellence in carrying out some aspect of the church's mission."

Strategy is figuring out how to get where we want to go. Where we generally want to go isn't that difficult because the components of thriving parishes are the same:

- vital worship that attracts and moves people;
- education and formation programs that transform lives;
- outreach efforts that make a difference;
- functional buildings that enable these activities; and
- sufficient financial resources to support all of the above.

The difficulty is figuring out what these five elements mean for a particular congregation. Strategic thinking means understanding exactly where you are and thinking both creatively and realistically about where it is possible to go in your particular circumstances. What would excellence look like? Strategic planning efforts fall short, first, because people are usually both unable and unwilling to see clearly their present situation, and second, because they don't think clearly about where they can actually go. Moreover, far too little effort is devoted to achieving excellence.

By "excellence" I don't mean any particular way of doing it. Excellent music does not necessarily entail a choir of men and boys, but neither excellence nor effectiveness can be achieved by following the path of least resistance. Whatever excellence looks like for you, it will come as a result of creative thought, disciplined planning, and hard work. So strategic thinking involves a close and dispassionate analysis of your current situation and its possibilities so that you understand who you are, where you are, where you want to go, and how you can get there. La Piana's book has resources that can guide you as you develop your leadership's capacity to think strategically.

Strategic thinking is required for leadership. Leadership is about moving the organization in a direction that will strengthen the organization. Leaders who don't think strategically may move the organization, but generally in ways that compromise its future. Thinking strategically will get the organization to a new place, and will get it there stronger than it was before.

Let's look at some examples where strategic thinking could have been useful.

One parish that had never had investments received a two million dollar bequest. Because they were completely unprepared for this windfall, they could not manage it well. Their annual giving fell by 30 percent and they were overspending the bequest to maintain an enhanced operation. Then the rector convinced the vestry to spend nearly half a million dollars to refurbish the parish house. When I questioned their thinking, the rector said, "Our plan is to find a tenant to provide income." I replied, "That's a wish, not a plan. A plan would have been to get a commitment from a tenant first. Then you would have borrowed against that lease and used the rent to pay off the debt."

In another church a successful thrift shop provided a large percentage of parish income. Those who ran the shop, many of whom were not parishioners, kept the rector and vestry on a fairly short leash while paying staff off the books and engaging in some other illegal or unbecoming practices. A series of priests let the situation go on, without getting the thrift shop under good management or breaking the parish's dependence on that income stream.

Elsewhere a beloved and long-serving rector steadfastly refused to introduce the 1979 Prayer Book during his tenure, which ended in the late 1990s. In so many ways he deserved the affection in which the parish held him, but he did them a grave disservice by keeping the old book, which was the path most congenial for him. His unwillingness to put the good of the parish above what he wanted has meant that the parish is still trying to recover from the many negative effects of his choice.

In each of these cases leaders did what was easiest and most comfortable for them but seriously weakened the parishes by not thinking about where their actions were taking the parish and what the effects might be. Thinking strategically will help your leadership leave the congregation stronger than it was when you became its leader.

GOVERNANCE AS THE WORK OF THE VESTRY

Every leader does leadership, and every leader works in the areas of development, fiduciary responsibilities, finances, personnel, and programs, but the vestry has certain priorities and the clergy others. The vestry's emphasis is on *governance*; the clergy's emphasis is on *management and operations*. Remember, here I am speaking in terms of the governance and operation of the institution, using secular terms on purpose. Education, pastoral care, and liturgy, for example, are essential parts of the operation and program of a parish church. That's why these things are by canon put under the control of the clergy. See how tradition and good institutional practice can mesh?

Fiduciary Responsibilities

The vestry's most important responsibility is to be the fiduciaries of the church's assets. In most parts of the country the members elect the vestry and wardens, but the vestry is the legal entity that holds title to the parish's assets in trust for the larger church. The vestry—comprised of the rector, churchwardens, and other members—are the fiduciaries, stewards, or trustees of the parish's real estate, money, buildings, furnishings, and fixtures. They hold title to these assets but they are not their rightful owners in the way we normally understand ownership. They received those assets into their care from their predecessors in office, and they have a responsibility to pass them on to their successors in a healthier condition than they were when they received them.

In the interests of good leadership vestries need to recover a sense of the gravity of these responsibilities. In legal terms fiduciaries, or trustees, have a "duty of care" because by definition they are entrusted with assets that belong to another. Yet many vestries, including those of large and historic parishes, make irresponsible decisions about the assets entrusted to them and are not held accountable. Some vestries sell property and use the proceeds of the sale to plug operating budget deficits. Others deplete endowments by overspending or by making poor investment decisions, thus breaking faith both with the past benefactors who gave the money and with future generations of parishioners that should have been able to benefit from those gifts. Vestries have been known to defer maintenance of the physical plants and pass on to their successors a crushing burden, or refuse to engage in stewardship formation and institutional fundraising, preferring to figure out how to get other people's money to pay as much as possible.

The idea of being a fiduciary is that you are *more* careful with the assets entrusted to you than you would be with your own. Yet vestry members frequently handle the church's assets with a nonchalance they would never bring to the management of their own money. You would not let your house deteriorate the way your church is, or spend your retirement savings on current bills just because it was easier than working. Becoming more aware of the solemn nature of your responsibilities as fiduciaries of assets that really belong to your successors is about building a better future for the church. Nor does it conflict with carrying out the mission of the church. Like a college, a museum, a hospital, or any other not-for-profit, you are managing money, real estate, and buildings so that you can accomplish your mission.

The most important items on the vestry's agenda are those that relate to its fiduciary role. These items include

- ensuring that real and financial assets are used prudently in support of the organization's mission, including an annual audit of the books;
- making prudent decisions regarding lease, mortgage, sale, or acquisition of real estate, including agreements for use of parish spaces by outside organizations;
- ensuring that resources are generated to keep the buildings in good repair;
- developing and approving human resources policies;
- dealing with legal issues, insurance, and other areas involving risk; recruiting potential candidates as future members of the vestry.

I wish it weren't necessary to mention one final aspect of the fiduciary role. If the ordained leader's work, or lack of it, is destroying the institution, it is the duty of the vestry to do what it can to address the situation. A vestry should not do this for frivolous reasons, such as simple disagreements or control issues. Nevertheless, when the priest's ministry has become so distorted or skewed that the witness and the very existence of the parish is threatened, it is the board's responsibility to take every action it can to save the parish.

The fiduciary responsibilities are the most important, and vestries should view the rest of their work through the lens of this role.

Personnel

Boards and vestries have an important but strictly limited role with regard to personnel: they call the rector or hire the executive director. It is a crucial role because leadership is crucial; it is limited because boards have no other staff decisions to make. The leader is responsible for all other staff. A wise rector will involve the personnel committee or the executive committee in the more important of these decisions, but the formal role of the vestry in personnel decisions is limited to decisions about the tenure of the priest in charge.

Many vestries do not do a good job selecting a leader, and some of the procedures judicatories and denominations recommend to congregations don't encourage them to look at this process in the right way. There is a longer discussion of hiring below in the section that deals with the clergy's responsibilities for personnel, but the short version is this: don't call somebody who fits a job description and don't hire by profile (young and married with two small children). As Jim Collins writes in *Good to Great*, "Whether someone is the 'right person' has more to do with character traits and innate capabilities than with specific knowledge, background, or skills."[2] Furthermore, doing a good job in finding the right person to be the ordained leader is sufficient. The vestry should not have control over the hiring, supervision, and dismissal of other staff.

Many vestries chafe at this limitation and want to insert themselves into the selection and supervision of the rest of the staff, but, in my experience, this is always unhealthy. Boards do governance; the executive director does management. Part of what you are looking for in a priest is someone who can manage the operation. This is not a specifically priestly task, but it is an essential task for someone who is in charge of a congregation, and lots of "otherworldly" priests do it quite well. You don't have to be a technocrat to be a good manager; you will do just fine if you practice mutual accountability. If the priest does a bad job at that, then it is just not going to work well no matter what the rest of the leadership tries to cobble together to make up for it.

Here is where the matter of trust comes in. In my observation, board involvement in personnel matters comes about because the leader is not handling the staff well, or at least in the way a group of board members wants it to be done. This inevitably leads to conflicts between vestry and priest and between vestry and employees, and it always causes low morale among the staff. Employees need to know to whom they report. They should report to the priest who is in charge, not to any lay leader or vestry committee. If need be, let such a committee counsel and coach the priest so he or she can do a better job.

The vestry's other responsibility with regard to personnel is to adopt personnel policies that are clear and fair. Churches in general fail to be good employers, especially when it comes to lay staff. Instead of thinking only of what you can afford, think for a minute about whether you would want to work for an organization that treated you the way you treat the lay employees of your parish. You may be a volunteer, but your employees are not, so compensation, vacation, and benefits policies should be fair. The Hebrew prophets' words about justice are directed at us as well.

Finances

Part of the vestry's role as financial overseers is to adopt policies that staff and volunteers follow as they handle what belongs to the church. Good internal controls are not a sign of a lack of trust; rather they protect not only the assets of the church but also those who are handling them. Good internal controls protect people from suspicion and, more importantly, they protect them from temptation. Canon Michael McPherson, the retired chief administrative officer of the Diocese of New York, frequently told lay leaders, "When people were asked why they had stolen from the church, the most common answer was, 'Because it was so easy.'" Lay people can misuse church money just as clergy can misuse their discretionary funds. We do everyone a service by creating a system in which misappropriation is not possible; it won't even occur to people to try to steal from such a system.

In the church in which I grew up, the financial secretary and his wife, who was the parish secretary, took the offering home, prepared the deposit, and updated the contribution records. This is not a good plan—counters should rotate, and all church records should be kept at the church. One parish learned the hard way when the widowed treasurer died alone at home and her apartment was sealed for weeks with no access to the checkbook or any financial records.

Vestries should receive a complete statement of year-to-date revenue and expenses compared to budget every month. Vestries need the answers to these questions:

- How are we doing so far this year?
- How does that compare with where we thought we would be?
- Are we ahead of or behind last year?
- What are our targets for the year?

This report should be in a format that can be understood and used, which means it should normally not exceed two pages, with similar items grouped together using bolded subtotals. In order to answer the above questions, four columns of numbers are needed:

- the current year-to-date figures;
- the budget to date;
- the previous year's results to date; and
- the total current year budget.

If the report is too long, or there are too many or too few columns, the vestry will not be able to get the answers it needs or it will get sidetracked into unimportant matters. Some vestries prefer to get sidetracked because it is easier to talk about the small numbers in the report than about the deficit or the fact that individual giving provides less than half of the operating budget. Complete reports that are designed to help the vestry answer the four questions above will go a long way to improving the discussion.

There should also be quarterly reports on the parish's investments. The purpose of these reports is to communicate the performance of the investments in percentage terms compared to appropriate benchmarks. Normally, even in bad economic times, these reports should not require a great deal of time. Assuming appropriate investment guidelines have been adopted, you just want to know how the portfolio is performing in relation to the benchmarks you've selected. You certainly don't want to try to rewrite your investment guidelines every meeting depending on market performance; the guidelines you've adopted are meant to shield you from emotional reactions to the ups and downs of the market.

Vestries cannot do their job if they don't receive monthly a revenue and expense statement and an investment report every quarter. If there is something—or more likely, someone—in your system that is preventing this information from reaching the vestry, it may not be something you can fix immediately. You may have to live with it for a while, but be quietly persistent in looking for opportunities to change things so that the vestry can learn to fulfill its fiduciary responsibilities with regard to the finances.

It is also the vestry's job to exercise financial leadership. Maybe your budget always has a deficit, or perhaps contributions are too small a percentage of your operating income. Maybe you are overspending your endowment. It is the vestry's job, with the full cooperation of the priest and the staff, to address these issues so the organization can move toward financial health.

It is not against the law for a not-for-profit to run a surplus every year. Indeed, the parish should at least break even or run a small surplus. Remember Charles Dickens' Mr. Micawber's rueful observation in *David Copperfield*: "Annual income twenty pounds, annual expenditure nineteen nineteen six, result happiness. Annual income twenty pounds, annual expenditure twenty pounds ought and six, result misery." If you keep running deficits, the money has to come from somewhere. Usually it comes from spending down your reserves or your endowment. This is unsustainable. If there aren't the ideas around the table for how the situation can be addressed, please find an outsider who can help. Your diocesan office may have someone who can work with you, or you can contact the Episcopal Church Foundation; their work in capital campaigns and planned giving has given them a great deal of expertise in church finances. You owe it to your future members to get this on track.

The final part of the vestry's financial role is to see that the books are audited and certified financial statements prepared. Again, there are many circumstances in which an audit may seem unnecessary, but my experience has caused me to place a high value on audits. The priest who was siphoning money into his personal account had the cooperation of the treasurer, after all— for years the two of them strenuously resisted an audit, claiming that it would be a poor use of the parish's money! Get a full audit, or at least comply with whatever the audit requirement of your diocese is. That is part of being accountable.

Development

I am using the word "development" in the sense it normally has in not-for-profits, which is securing the financial resources the institution needs to thrive. Vestries have an opportunity to help the parish think and talk about money in a healthy way. Certainly this means participating in the annual pledge drive. I recommend the practice of some parishes in which the entire leadership—clergy, wardens, vestry, treasurer—make their pledges for the following year before soliciting pledges from the congregation. Announce that the entire leadership has pledged, and announce the number of those pledges and the amount those pledges total.

This kind of transparency will help people understand that money is not a shameful thing for churches to discuss. A rector was nearly thrown out of one parish for printing an alphabetical list of those who pledged in the newsletter in order to thank them; naturally it was the non-pledgers who were mortally offended. We can attend a concert by the local choral society in our church on Saturday evening and note with equanimity how people are thanked as sponsors, patrons, friends, and so on according to how much they gave. If anything is brought up in church the next morning about the amount people give, however, look out. Part of the vestry's job is to help this discussion be more rational. A parish in one of the richest communities in the New York area for years began every annual pledge appeal by apologizing for bringing up money, but those who tithe or who give some other percentage off the top aren't usually very defensive about speaking of their giving.

The vestry also needs to think about developing other sources of income, for the operating budget or capital purposes or outreach. Most parishes are woefully underfunded. Individual giving on the whole is far short of what it could be, and parishes often do not identify or maximize the revenue they might obtain from other sources, such as grants or revenues derived from the use of their buildings.

Fairs, thrift shops, rummage sales, dinners—it is a healthy sign when some activities like these are occurring regularly, especially if at least part of the money raised goes to outreach. Grants are also available for certain purposes. But here it is important not to sit on the sidelines, so don't suggest that a thrift shop is a good idea for others to work on. If you suggest applying for a grant, be willing to do some research and to help write the proposal. The point here is that vestries need to be accountable as well. I've witnessed several vestry meetings where a member has blamed others for not following up on her idea about organizing a fundraising event that she herself was not willing to work on.

Programs

The vestry's principal responsibility for programs is simply to know what they are and to ensure that they are consonant with the parish's identity and mission. That is the *governance* function with respect to programs. Members of the vestry will probably be involved in designing and running programs, but that kind of management is not the responsibility of the vestry as a group. I don't mean that the vestry should be silent when the priest is reporting on the adult education program. No doubt she would be happy to hear ideas about what might make that program more compelling or logistically smoother, but that is different from the vestry trying to run it.

What causes most of the confusion between the role of the governing board and the role of the staff in most small and medium-sized parishes is the fact that members of the vestry are likely to be some of the principal volunteer "staff." As volunteers they are part of the team that works with the clergy and lay staff to organize and implement the programs, yet they will also be among the people for whom the program is organized. At vestry meetings, however, the volunteers and participants wear a different hat. Let the discussions at the vestry meetings be limited to the governance and informational functions outlined above; let the management and operational discussions happen at other times. It will make your vestry meetings shorter and more effective, and it will reduce frictions.

MANAGEMENT AS THE WORK OF THE ORDAINED "EXECUTIVE DIRECTOR"

The priest works in the same areas as the vestry, but with different priorities and different duties.

Personnel

An important part of leadership—and certainly the most important part of management—is staff selection and oversight. There is quite a bit to say about this because it matters so much. In the first place, having the right staff is essential to effective ministry. Even the smallest churches need competent musicians and some way of keeping the buildings clean and in repair. In my estimation too many congregations have accepted inadequate staffing patterns as inevitable (no secretary and an eight-hour-a-week sexton) instead of developing the resources to staff the place properly. In this situation too much of the energy of clergy and membership is focused literally on housekeeping matters, without enough left over to do the work of the church. Setting up or acquiescing to a situation where there is no money or energy to do more than the weekly services makes the parish less of a church.

Even in small and medium-sized places, the members of the staff, who may be volunteers, are the foundation on which programs are built. The staff is the framework that supports the mission. The feeding program is effective and keeps growing because the buildings are open, clean and set up, and there is someone to help carry things. Someone in the office is helping to coordinate the volunteers and the supplies; someone else is doing the paperwork for grants. The vestry doesn't have to spend time figuring out how some repair can be done; instead, the minutes can note the vestry's thanks to the sexton.

You might be thinking, "But we can't afford staff!" And you're right—with your current levels of funding you can't afford staff. Your members are not giving enough, and you don't have other sources of income. But is that how it has to be? Below we will discuss your role in developing resources for the institution. I am convinced that many situations have possibilities for increased revenue that are not being tapped.

Problems with staff are generally the result of bad management—not always, but usually. If you ever need to terminate someone you have hired, there has been a failure on your part. Staff problems develop because the wrong person was hired, or you micromanaged, or you didn't pay enough attention, or you destroyed morale by not listening to or trusting the staff, or you let a situation slide without oversight or intervention until it got messy.

If staff members are volunteers, there are additional shoals to navigate. In some instances the volunteer is more committed to having the position than to doing the job, but more frequently, especially in smaller places, too much is loaded onto the backs of just a few volunteers. This can lead to an unfair situation where someone is being exploited. It can also lead to one person's unhealthy ownership of large parts of parish life. That is why it is a good idea to try to speak of these possibilities frankly, up front, so that people volunteer for the jobs they want to do at a sustainable and healthy level.

There are five essential principles to follow in effective staff management:

- get the right people on board;
- don't let process trump results;
- find a way to replace the wrong people;
- give and solicit constant feedback; and
- support the staff at all times.

Get the right people on board. In a chapter entitled, "First Who… Then What," Jim Collins makes the perhaps counter-intuitive claim that it is necessary to "get the right people on the bus" before deciding where the bus is going.[3] Most of the time we are encouraged to do it the other way around, to figure out what we want a job to be, write a job description, and find someone whose qualifications and experience fit the position. Collins's way is much healthier. The right people always bring more with them than the ability to do the work in a job description. Get the right people, and encourage them to take the job where they can. The job you wanted to get done will get done, and so will a lot more. Let the right person fit the job to himself; don't try to fit the right person into a pre-determined slot.

The right person needs to be competent in the core functions of the job—musician, administrator, maintenance person, program director—but competence isn't the primary factor in hiring. The right person may actually have no experience in certain parts of the job but will learn to do it, and in the process will give you far more than you expected.

So when you interview, you want to gauge basic ability and willingness to do the job, but you are also trying to find out what engages the person, what make her light up or what drives him crazy. As far as you can tell, is this someone you will look forward to seeing every day, someone you will be able to talk things over with, someone you won't have to manage around, someone who will make it possible for you to do your job better? So try to have more of a conversation than an interview. Ask questions that are really open and let the person speak and tell her story.

If you possibly can, speak to every qualified person who applies. It will help you see the directions in which different people could take the position. When you have it down to two or three, I have found it helpful to have a number of lay leaders interview those finalists without me. I've learned a lot from the discussions that follow and have made better decisions because of them.

When you arrive in a new position, you may find a parishioner already on the staff, or one who may want to apply for a position when one becomes available. Many people say that hiring parishioners is a problem; I believe that hiring the wrong parishioner is a problem, just as hiring the wrong non-parishioner is a problem. I have seen numerous situations in which a parishioner rendered superlative service in a paid position. Rules of thumb can be useful guides if they are applied with flexibility, but if rigidly followed they will give you the illusion of certainty around a question where certainty is not available. It is messy to hire the wrong parishioner, but that should not stop you from hiring the right person, even if that person is a member of your congregation.

Finally, take the time to find the right person. Do not hire the wrong person just because you haven't found the right person yet. It is better to go for a little while longer without filling the job, and you will be glad you waited.

Don't let process trump results. When the right person does present herself, don't allow process to get in the way of the right outcome. Don't let the right person get away. This is tricky because high-handed actions on the part of the leader are to be avoided; the watchwords are consultation, consensus (if possible), and mutual accountability. However, if somebody you know to be the right person wants to get on your bus, I think you owe it to the institution you lead to figure out a way to get that person on board.

Here is what happened to me in the spring of 2008. A few minutes before the eight o'clock service, an Altar Guild member said there was somebody who wanted to talk to me. As clergy know, that means you're about to get hit up for money—and, sure enough, a man in his thirties told me he had come to New York two weeks before and had not been able to find a job. He needed money, and he wanted to work.

"I can't do anything about work right now because I have to start the mass," I told him, "but if you need money, here's $40." He turned and walked a few steps away from me. I went over to him, and he was crying, and said, "I don't want it that way. I want to work." After the mass I found some things for him to do so that I could pay him, and in five or six hours he accomplished several tasks requiring a wide diversity of skills. The sexton and myself, along with a few others who had seen him work, agreed that this man should not get away. Our physical plant was enormous; a dozen maintenance staff were needed. The church was strapped, so I told the man that I would pay him personally until I could figure out how the church could hire him.

Our regular sexton did not want to work fulltime, so by finagling some numbers I figured out how we could pay for a fulltime and a part-time position without spending more than we were already paying for one fulltime position. Within a few weeks, after a background check and other procedures, I got the vestry to agree that the new man could move into a derelict apartment in the complex with the agreement that he would, apart from his regular work, fix up the apartment.

What I did left a bad taste in some people's mouths, and I could understand why. On the other hand, I somehow knew that it was important for us to have that particular person working for us. Over time, events proved me correct. In addition to working skillfully and hard, the man developed a substantial new income stream for the church by managing the rental of some spaces for private parties and dances. He also made several remarkable musical contributions to some special services.

I am not offering this as a template for how to act all the time; in fact part of me is still uncomfortable with the actions I took. If I'd been on the vestry, I'm sure I would have been among those who objected to what I did. On the other hand, the result was indisputably right. This may have been an example of Bonhoeffer's "responsible action" where we act from our own inner principles and without any assurance that we are right. Perhaps it shows that leadership is a craft, not a set of rules. Or maybe it was something I shouldn't have done.

Find a way to replace the wrong people. The corollary of getting the right people on board is, unfortunately, getting the wrong people off. This is not easily done in most parishes, and that is a good thing even though it will drive you crazy to have the wrong people working for you.

If you are walking into a situation where there has been bad leadership, the staff and volunteers will be affected by the resulting dysfunction. When good people who are committed to the mission of the organization have to work for bad leaders, they become part of a culture they may not be able to let go of. When staff members become skilled at covering up, enabling, hiding information, and engaging in the kinds of other behavior necessary in those situations, they may not be able to change when the leadership changes. They may need a different employment situation in order to regain the health that the bad situation took from them. This is unfortunate, because bad leaders often have very good people working for them. Ruining the right people is one of the most regrettable things bad leaders do. Work hard with people in those situations and see if it's possible for them to re-adapt to a healthier dynamic. If that is not possible, you won't do them or the parish any favors by keeping them in that situation.

If your predecessor was a good, or at least a decent, leader, chances are you don't have any staff members who need to be replaced. Be very careful in your evaluation of those working for the parish so that you do not delude yourself, keeping in mind the priest who didn't want any "stars" in his administration. Is the parish administrator really the wrong person for the job, or is she someone whose abilities intimidate you? Did some misguided mentor tell you that you need to get new people in who will be loyal only to you?

In other words, do not let your baggage get in the way of your estimation of the fitness of the staff. And remember, if you're the right kind of leader, you don't want staff members who are loyal to you; you want staff that are loyal to the institution and to its mission. They will also be fiercely devoted to you because you support them so they can give their best, and you let them know that they are an important part of the institution's success.

Regardless of your predecessor's competence, you will, almost certainly, encounter lay leaders with unhealthy ownership and control issues. Chances are that you will have to live with such situations far longer than you want to even if they irritate other lay people as well. You will probably not be able to unseat them. The members of a parish have deep and complex ties that predate your arrival and will continue when you are gone. The job of the leader is not to chase difficult people away. The priest in Chapter 2 who took seven years to move his parish from Morning Prayer to the Holy Eucharist took as his watchword, "I did not lose a single one of those whom you gave me" (John 18:9). Another capable priest has created such a culture of health in the parish he serves that several people who thrive on conflict have had to seek elsewhere to find it.

It takes a great deal of energy and a combination of tactics to deal with such situations. You will make missteps, but if you remember that you may not be right and hold yourself account-able to those you lead, those errors are unlikely to be fatal.

The rest of what I want to say with regard to staff supervision assumes that you have the right people working for you, for there simply is no way to manage or supervise the wrong person into doing a good job.

Give and solicit constant feedback. Evaluation should not be something that happens only once a year. Part of being a good manager is making sure staff members know at all times where they stand, and to make sure they know where you stand with them. If you have the right people working for you, this will con-sist primarily of thanking them at least daily for the good work they are doing.

Your job as a supervisor is to create the best conditions you can for your staff to work. Observe what staff members are doing and listen to how they talk about their jobs. Consider whether there are things you can do to make their work easier and more efficient. Offer your ideas to them for their consider-ation but make sure they are comfortable in telling you whether they think your ideas will work or not. This is important. Staff members who want to work hard and oblige you will sometimes take a tentative suggestion on your part as a directive. Make sure you tell them that they know more about their jobs than you do, so they need to tell you if something you have floated won't work.

When something goes wrong, address the situation immedi-ately, but make sure you address it this way. First, tell the staff member that you know he meant to do the right thing in the right way. Second, assure him that if something went wrong, it's almost surely a problem with the system, not with the individual. Then figure out together how to fix the system. There is prob-ably a change you can make in your procedures that will keep the problem from recurring. Regardless of the reason, because you have the right people working for you, they will feel badly that something went wrong and will apologize. Apologize to them in return for not having thought sooner about how to make your systems more failsafe.

If you do it this way, there will be no surprises at the annual evaluation time. Rather, it will be an opportunity to remember successes and failures in an easy and open way. It will be a time to talk about what changes you can make that will make the staff member better able to do his job. Most of all, it will be a time to say thank you.

Support the staff at all times. If you have the right people and you want people to give their best to their work, you must make sure they know that you have their back with respect to other employees, members of the parish, and members of the public. You don't need to make them show deference to you, nor do you need to throw your weight around. You're already at the top of the heap. They know who is in charge. They may not know, however, how important they are to you and to the organization. Your job is to make the people who work for you know how much you respect and value them.

Remember at all times that these are the people who make it possible for you to do your job. You and the mission of the institution are dependent on them, not the other way around, which is why staff management is your highest priority. That is why it is worth all the time and thought it takes to do the job of supervision right.

Sticking up for your staff does not mean ignoring complaints from others. It does mean, however, that you will not automatically assume that the complainant is correct and the staff member is culpable. In many instances, you'll know what the person is complaining about and be able to clear up a misunderstanding. Maybe you'll apologize because the oversight was a result of a system failure that you intend to address. If you don't know what the situation is, tell whoever is complaining that you'll look into it, but that you are sure there is a misunderstanding or a reasonable explanation because you know the staff person wants to do the right thing in the right way.

Then go to the staff member and talk about it in the way outlined above. If there is something that needs to be corrected, correct it. If there was a serious mistake or oversight the staff member may need to apologize to whoever had the problem, but don't humiliate anyone or to let a lay leader throw his weight around or bully the staff.

Here is an example of what *not* to do. In one diocese with an outreach program to which many contributed, one donor e-mailed the bishop complaining that her contribution had been returned to her with a note saying they didn't know what it was for. The bishop copied the finance office staff on the reply, thus letting them know that it was up to them to prove themselves innocent. After several hours of consternation, somebody asked if the contribution had actually been sent to the diocesan office. As it turned out, the check had been addressed to some other church institution—but even so, neither the bishop nor the individual apologized. Of course the staff felt demoralized, and not only for the rest of the day. Such things have long-term effects.

If you have the right people, trust them. If a problem of staff trustworthiness does arise, it needs to be resolved as quickly as possible in one of two ways. If indeed the staff person cannot be trusted, it is necessary to get rid of her. If, however, the problem is your suspicious or controlling nature, you need to deal with that yourself. That is your problem, not hers. In any case, problems of trust must be solved immediately. Do not treat the staff with constant suspicion. It is completely demoralizing.

Nor should you play power games with the staff. They do not need to be reminded who is in charge. If there is a lay leader that wants to show he is in charge by badmouthing the staff, call him on that inappropriate behavior and do not allow it to continue. In like manner, if a lay leader tells you that you have taken the wrong approach to a staff issue, please listen to that possibly valuable feedback.

Programs

If you are in charge of the congregation, you are responsible for its program life—liturgy, pastoral care, education and formation, and outreach. You don't have to do it all, but you do need to see that it gets done to the extent possible, given the congregation's circumstances. In an ideal world, this is where you can spend the bulk of your time. What drew you to ordination was probably the desire to lead worship, teach, counsel, and serve those in need. The purpose of this section is not to give ideas for programs, but to suggest a few ideas to help guide your stewardship of the parish program.

When you first come to a church, you'll find some kind of program cycle in place. There are likely to be some things that people want to continue to do but seem less vital or don't appear to be working very well. There may be other parts of the cycle that you don't like much. I made a special point above saying that you, not the vestry, are responsible for the programmatic life of the congregation. While that is still true, I will now add that *the program life of the congregation belongs fundamentally to the congregation.*

You are responsible for the liturgy, for example, but that does not mean it is appropriate for you to conduct it however you prefer. The congregation predates you and will be there when you leave. There certainly are times when it is necessary to make a big change, as when a new prayer book is introduced, and we do have a responsibility to see that the parish's worship is not too eccentric or far from the mainstream. All the same, in general I believe it's good for the parish and good for the humility and strength of our leadership to respect the congregation's customs and preferences.

The same restraint needs to characterize your stewardship of the rest of the parish program. Maybe new life can be breathed into some of the activities that people like that have lost their vitality; perhaps parts of the program structure can be kept with new content or a new emphasis. Beware of the urge to remake it all in your image. For example, some clergy who like to maintain control think up hoops people must jump through in order to participate fully in parish life. The rector of one parish likes the Alpha program, for example, so all couples who want to get married in that parish must complete the ten-week program as part of their marriage preparation. In another parish the priest required those wishing to get married to attend church and pledge for one year. Only one couple agreed to those terms. A lay leader was speaking approvingly of this requirement when I asked, "Did they remain part of the parish?" "No," she replied, "but they came

for that year." Other priests place substantial requirements on
parents wishing to have their children baptized. Some parishes
have been thrown into turmoil because the rector changed the
age at which he would prepare young people for confirmation.
One rector told the members of the choir that they should cease
being part of it unless they felt a clear call from God to continue;
another wanted all those standing for election to the vestry to
have participated in a Cursillo weekend.

These requirements may be within the canonical rights of the
clergy to impose, though I think setting requirements for vestry
service beyond what is spelled out in the legal documents is probably not enforceable. Let's leave aside the more idiosyncratic
requirements and think a bit about requiring either participation
in some program or church attendance for some period of time in
order to be married or have children baptized. Why do you want
to impose these requirements? Of what actual benefit will they be
either to the individuals or to the parish?

Alpha and Cursillo are programs of recent origin that work
for some, but not for others. In some parishes where the rector
has championed such programs, the internal dynamics of the
congregation have become skewed. An in-group is created.
Committed members who haven't done Cursillo are inadver-
tently or intentionally made to feel less a part of the parish.
You would think there would have to be some pretty substantial
benefits to make that a price worth paying, but the parishes I
know of that require Alpha or Cursillo, or set a high bar for
marriages and baptisms, are not growing faster than other
congregations. They seem rather to be part of a general decline,
especially since, as pointed out in Chapter 1, rule-based religion is generally unattractive. I also am not aware that couples
required to attend church before marriage or baptism are more
likely to become active members of the congregation. And does
it serve a valid purpose to fight with parents over the age at
which their children are confirmed?

If you are convinced in your own mind that you have the right
to impose these things, nonetheless insisting rather than simply
inviting indicates a need for control that is worth examining.

Make your case and encourage the parish to do what you think works best, but remember that yours is not the only way. Go ahead and figure out a way to prepare the eleven-year-old for confirmation even though the rest of the class is sixteen or seventeen. The lesson people take away from examples of selfless leadership like these will be more life-changing than the confirmation curriculum that can be used only with older teenagers.

Development

Part of your job is securing the resources the parish needs. Money is not just the laity's job, as some clergy prefer to believe. The executive director of every not-for-profit spends a fair amount of time thinking about where and how to get money and then getting it. You may be able to avoid this if you want to, but you will leave your successor an institution weaker than it could have been and have shirked an important part of your job.

Getting money takes work, whether it is developing a new income stream by making your space available for new activities or figuring out what grants you qualify for and applying for them. It can, however, be very rewarding. Because of your creative work in developing a possibility for a new income line or a grant, the parish is able to accomplish the long-desired goal of refurbishing the gymnasium or hiring a sexton. Looking to future goals is also part of your responsibility. What would appropriate staffing for your size and type of congregation look like? How much should you be putting aside in a capital reserve fund every year for building maintenance? These are not the questions you feel like asking when the budget is short and you're lurching from one building crisis to another, but we tend to make progress in the areas in which we intend to make progress. What will help us is to keep these things in mind, so that when something comes up, we can look to see whether there is anything that can help move us in the direction in which we intend to go. There may indeed be situations in which little can be done, but often the main reason is that the leaders of the congregation have decided that in advance.

So here are some ways to increase the amount available for the congregation's operation:

- increased annual giving based on percentage giving off the top;
- a planned giving program to build an endowment;
- grants for programs;
- capital fundraising that relieves the operating budget of paying for capital needs; and
- new income from rentals or programs.

There is almost certainly something that can be done. It will take work, it may upset some established patterns, and ultimately it will be good for the parish.

Finances

As the head of the operation, your principal job with respect to finances is to make sure the operation stays within its budget, assuming that the budget is realistic. You also have a responsibility to see that the bookkeeping and accounting functions are set up and conducted in ways that make an audit as straightforward and helpful as possible. Implement the internal controls approved by the vestry. It protects everyone.

As chair of the governing board, moreover, you will want to make sure that

- the vestry receives the reports it needs;
- the reports are clear, complete, and concise;
- the vestry understands the reports; and
- the discussion of the reports focuses on matters of significance.

You need to make sure that the vestry exercises financial leadership as outlined above. Does annual giving provide a healthy percentage of operating income? Is the endowment managed well in an arm's-length relationship? Is the total amount drawn from the endowment each year sustainable over the long term? Are sources of income beyond the gifts of the congregation being sought with appropriate creativity? You probably did not get ordained in order to deal with finances, but I hope you'll see how important this is to the effectiveness of the rest of your ministry.

Fiduciary Responsibilities

As *executive director*, your role is first to make sure the board is fully aware of situations that touch upon their fiduciary responsibilities and, second, to see that the board's decisions are implemented. As *chair of the governing board*, your duty is to help the members of the board understand that exercising their fiduciary responsibilities is their most important function. If they fail to be good stewards of the money, the land, and the buildings, it won't matter much what they spent their time doing instead.

"THINK YOUR LIFE THROUGH FROM ITS END"

William Gladstone was the Liberal prime minister under Queen Victoria and a great churchman. The son of a close friend approached him one day seeking advice regarding his career plans.

"First," the young man explained, "I plan to complete my studies at Oxford."

"Splendid," replied Gladstone. "And what then?"

"Well, sir, I then plan to study law and become a prominent barrister."

"Excellent. And what then?"

"Then I plan to stand for election and become a Member of Parliament."

"Wonderful. And what then?"

"Then, sir, I plan to rise to prominence in the party and be appointed to a cabinet post."

"A worthy ambition. And what then?"

"Oh, Mr. Gladstone," the boy said a bit self-consciously, "I hope one day to become prime minister and serve my country with the same distinction as you."

"A noble desire, young man. And what then?"

"Well, sir, I expect that in time I will be forced to retire from public life."

"You will indeed. And what then?"

Puzzled by the question, the young man said hesitatingly, "I expect then that one day I will die."

"Yes, you will, and what then?"

"I don't know, sir! I haven't thought any further than that."

"Young man," said Gladstone, "you are a fool. Go home and think your life through from its end."

When I was a child, mazes were part of the puzzle books that I played with. I discovered that mazes were easier to solve if I started at the end and worked back to the beginning. I used to wonder uneasily if that were cheating, so I was relieved to read the story about Gladstone. It is possible to take many wrong turns in our lives that lead us to painful and frustrating dead ends, but it's much less likely that we will take those turns if we have thought through our lives from their end.

The point of the story is that in every area of life, you need to know where you want to end up in order to figure out how to begin and what to do. If you are designing a computer database, you need to know how you will want to pull the information out in order to know how to enter it in. Every aspect of an accounting system needs to be designed with the annual audit in mind. To figure out the deadline for the newsletter, you need to start with the date you want it to go out and work backwards. We may know that this is necessary with deadlines and databases, but we are seldom trained to think that way about our lives and ministries.

Where do we want the institution to be when we go? What do we want to be remembered for? What legacy will we hand to those who come after us? We might as well be intentional about these questions. After all, we will be remembered for something, so why shouldn't it be what we want it to be?

Probably we would really rather not be remembered for the kinds of things for which weak, arrogant, and ineffective leaders are remembered. We don't want to be remembered for making the institution stumble, for being insensitive or self-involved, for depleting the endowment, or letting the buildings crumble. Nor do we want to be remembered as being overly concerned with our compensation, with how others defer to us, or with the trappings of office. We don't want to be remembered for our addictions or for what we hid during our tenure. When we are gone, it will all come out. If we have been covering up some negative aspects of our stewardship of the parish, they will be revealed as soon as we take our smoke and mirrors away with us. We might as well think our ministry and our leadership through from their end.

What do you want your legacy to be? I don't think you can ask yourself that question without realizing the extent to which selflessness is necessary even to deal with the question. Oddly, if your legacy is to be a constructive one, it is fundamentally not about you. The legacy you want to leave is going to consist of things like a stronger parish life, functional buildings, a culture of trust and generosity. To be remembered only for your wit or your way with the liturgy is not a legacy; you will take your humor and your dashing style with you when you go. You will leave behind an institution that is weaker or stronger as a result of your work, an institution better or worse able to meet the challenges it faces after your departure.

In one parish the enormous buildings had been neglected for decades. The few repairs there were had been done in the most slapdash way. My goal was to fix whatever was broken and to do it in a way congruent with the beauty and quality of the church. The sexton told me that he had become accustomed to shutting off whatever broke and that it required a different mindset to think about fixing it instead. When we planned any repair, including what colors to paint, we applied the "successor test": would our successors thank us for doing the repair in this way or would they mutter, "What were those people thinking?"

If we think our minstry through beginning with the end, we will understand that only leadership that is humble, strong, and mutually accountable will get the institutions we serve from where they are to where we want them to go.

May you and I both become that kind of leader.

End Notes:

1. David La Piana, *The Nonprofit Strategy Revolution* (St. Paul, MN: Fieldstone Alliance, 2008), 31.
2. Ibid, 64.
3. Ibid, 41–64.

SUGGESTED READING

Argyris, Chris. *Overcoming Organizational Defenses: Facilitating Organizational Learning.* Boston: Allyn and Bacon, 1990.
_____. *Flawed Advice and the Management Trap: How Managers Can Know When They're Getting Good Advice and When They're Not.* New York: Oxford University Press, 2000.

Collins, Jim. *Good to Great: Why Some Companies Make the Leap... and Others Don't.* New York: HarperCollins, 2001.
_____. *Good to Great and the Social Sectors: A Monograph to Accompany Good to Great.* New York: HarperCollins, 2005.

Drucker, Peter F. *Managing the Nonprofit Organization: Principles and Practices.* New York: Collins Business, 2005.

Freeman, Lindsay Hardin, ed. *Doing Holy Business: The Best of Vestry Papers.* New York: Church Publishing, 2006.

Friedman, Edwin H. *Generation to Generation: Family Process in Church and Synagogue.* New York: The Guilford Press, 1985.

Friedman Edwin H., Margaret M. Treadwell, and Edward W. Beal. *A Failure of Nerve: Leadership in the Age of the Quick Fix.* New York: Seabury Books, 2007.

Godin, Seth. *The Dip: A Little Book that Teaches You When to Quit (and When to Stick).* New York: Penguin Group, 2007.

Greenleaf, Robert K. *Servant Leadership: A Journey into the Nature of Legitimate Power and Greatness.* New York/Mahwah NJ: Paulist Press, 2002.

Heifetz, Ronald A. and Marty Linsky. *Leadership on the Line: Staying Alive through the Dangers of Leading.* Boston: Harvard Business School Press, 2002.

Hoge, Dean R. and Jacqueline E. Wenger. *Pastors in Transition: Why Clergy Leave Local Church Ministry.* Grand Rapids: Eerdmans, 2005.

La Piana, David. *The Nonprofit Strategy Revolution: Real-Time Strategic Planning in a Rapid-Response World.* St. Paul MN: Fieldstone Alliance, 2008.

Lehr, Fred. *Clergy Burnout: Recovering from the 70-Hour Work Week...and Other Self-Defeating Practices.* Minneapolis: Augsburg Fortress Press, 2006.

Martin, Kevin E. *The Myth of the 200 Barrier: How to Lead Through Transitional Growth.* Nashville: Abingdon Press, 2005.

McIntosh, Gary L. and Samuel D. Rima. *Overcoming the Dark Side of Leadership: How to Become an Effective Leader by Confronting Potential Failures.* Revised edition. Grand Rapids: Baker Books, 2007.

Morse, MaryKate. *Making Room for Leadership: Power, Space and Influence.* Downers Grove IL: IVP Books, 2008.

Seidman, Dov. *How: Why HOW We Do Anything Means Everything...in Business (and in Life).* Hoboken NJ: John Wiley & Sons, Inc., 2007.

Zinni, Tony and Tony Koltz. *Leading the Charge: Leadership Lessons from the Battlefield to the Boardroom.* New York: Palgrave Macmillan, 2009.